brilliant

ssertiveness

brilliant

assertiveness

What the most assertive people know, do and say

Dannie Lu Carr

PEARSON

Harlow, England • London • New York • Boston • San Francisco • Toronto • Sydney • Auckland • Singapore • Hong Kong
Tokyo • Seoul • Taipei • New Delhi • Cape Town • São Paulo • Mexico City • Madrid • Amsterdam • Munich • Paris • Milan

PEARSON EDUCATION LIMITED

Edinburgh Gate
Harlow CM20 2JE
Tel: +44 (0)1279 623623
Fax: +44 (0)1279 431059
Website: www.pearson.com/uk

First published in Great Britain in 2012

© Dannie Lu Carr 2012

Pearson Education is not responsible for the content of third-party internet sites.

ISBN: 978-0-273-76867-8

British Library Cataloguing-in-Publication Data
A catalogue record for this book is available from the British Library

Library of Congress Cataloging-in-Publication Data
Carr, Dannie Lu.
   Brilliant assertiveness : what the most assertive people know, do, and say / Dannie Lu Carr. -- 1st ed.
      p. cm.
   Includes index.
   ISBN 978-0-273-76867-8 (pbk.)
   1. Assertiveness (Psychology) I. Title.
   BF575.A85C37 2012
   158.2--dc23
                        2012009280

10 9 8 7 6 5 4 3 2 1
16 15 14 13 12

Cartoons by Bill Piggins
Typeset in 10/14pt Plantin by 3
Printed in Great Britain by Henry Ling Ltd., at the Dorset Press, Dorchester, Dorset

Contents

About the author

Dannie Lu Carr is a communications consultant, specialising in assertiveness, creative thinking, problem solving, change management, presentation and pitching. Her work has included speaking, coaching and presenting for a wide range of organisations in the business, education and charity worlds.

She is a consultant and trainer with the London-based communications company Impact Factory, which specialises in a diverse range of training from leadership to presentation, where she has worked extensively with many international businesses on a range of different issues.

All of her work is centred around empowering the individual or team by looking at everyday matters such as confidence, communication and creative thinking. Her approach is realistic, down-to-earth and supportive, while really getting to the core of key issues.

Dannie also works as a writer, director, actor, voiceover artist and acting coach.

Acknowledgements

Jo Ellen Grzyb, Robin Chandler and all at Impact Factory for their knowledge, wisdom, experience and support.

David Bliss for being my friend through the toughest times, always the voice of reason and a solid reality-checkpoint.

Neil McGuigan and the team at Revolution Personal Training Studios in Angel for pushing my fitness to its limit, listening to my babble and making me laugh so much.

Jacq, for the wonderful opportunity and those invaluable notes.

My family.

Introduction

Imagine this ... you get everything you want in life.

Sounds good doesn't it? What does it mean?

Well, imagine that you're perfectly happy to ask for what you want. It wouldn't occur to you not to. It is second nature to you. You set your own priorities and stick to them. You decide what you do with your own money, time and energy. And if anyone challenges you, you handle their questions with confidence and ease.

What's more, if life hurls a curve ball your way you face those challenges and risks knowing that you feel utterly capable of handling them and you take risks to find solutions.

You're also happy asking for what you need without apologising for it. You have the choice as to whether you speak up or not in response to situations.

Your self-esteem is wholly intact.

As a result you are happier, more successful and clear about your direction in work and in life. You stand up for what you believe in and people respect you for it.

Sounds really good doesn't it? In fact, it almost sounds too good to be true, wouldn't you agree? Surely only innately confident, happy people achieve this?

Well no. It's what assertive people experience everyday. And the good news is that anyone can learn to be assertive. It's simply a matter of giving yourself the head space to achieve it and working honestly with yourself. And, let's face it, you're worth that. Right?

Assertiveness isn't a rigid set of rules, it's about the state of mind you actively choose. The skills of assertiveness can be adapted to suit your personality, to suit what you feel comfortable doing and saying in the particular situation you find yourself.

So think of the term 'assertiveness' as being a flexible spectrum of behaviour, rather than something fixed that you either do or do not achieve. What we are working with throughout this book are endless choices and many degrees of variation within them.

And what we're really looking at is tweaking your behaviour so that you can achieve that persona imagined at the start of the introduction. As with any behavioural change, it isn't enough to be aware of how to do it, you have to actually take the plunge and do it.

Why we act the way we do

Here's the science bit. The way we respond in situations is governed by a complex set of feelings, thoughts and behaviours, which are all inherently linked. We react in the ways that our brain thinks are most useful. Sadly, however, these reactions are often governed by how we have been conditioned by our life experiences. This means that sometimes we can get into the pattern of not always opting for the most useful response.

To understand why this happens we need to take a quick trip down memory lane. As we grow up, various things happen to us, good and bad, and we respond to them in various ways. As each experience happens, our brain codes it and stores it up as a type of behaviour. At its simplest, if we touch something hot and burn ourselves the brain says 'let's not do that again'. The same mechanism works for more complex issues – how we dealt with the school bully, with rejection by a friend or love interest, or how we accepted praise or success. Every facet of human life is coded by the brain so that the next time the situation arises the brain offers us a short cut to how we should respond.

The bully at school drove us to hide away from them … so guess what? The bully at work will have the same result! The hard work we did on our school project got us the acclaim of an admired teacher … so, of course, we strive for high performance to gain that same acclaim from our peers throughout life.

It's a clever system and without it we'd find day-to-day life very difficult. But you need to be aware that the way you think, feel and behave is not set in stone, it's just a code, and if it's not working in your favour you can change it, with a bit of willpower and patience. Once your brain grasps this, it will also grasp that it's important to stay curious and question regularly how you are responding to things, otherwise you risk getting stuck in behaviours that aren't very helpful to you yet again.

The really good news is that you can help your brain to develop better bits of code, and once they are stored in your subconscious you'll see how much power you have to make decisions about how you want to react to the circumstances in which you find yourself.

In life we can all get 'stuck' if we stay only with the theory of how we would like things to change, so it is crucial that you also begin to practise doing things differently so that the body gets it on a behavioural level. It's almost like developing a new muscle memory of how to respond.

brilliant impact

As soon as you start to become assertive in your life, even in small ways, everything begins to shift. Suddenly there is a smile on your face, clarity in your mind, a spring in your step and everyone wanting whatever it is that you've got! Being assertive and taking charge is a pleasant and empowering place to be.

How this book works

Part 1 of this book will explore what assertiveness really means in the world at large and why assertiveness is the best position to operate from. It will also look at how social conditioning through childhood, adolescence and adulthood has an effect on people's behavioural patterns, and how that can result in the ability or inability to be assertive in different situations. For example, some people are assertive at home but struggle at work while others are the reverse. Keep in mind here that, while there are a few exceptional people who are assertive all the time, most of us struggle at some point and there are numerous reasons why, which Part 1 of the book will make clear.

Part 2 offers some practical tips, tools, techniques and exercises that will enable you to be more assertive. These exercises will help you understand the components of what makes up assertive behaviour and how you can adjust them, sometimes in a very small and simple way, to make them work for you positively and productively.

The last chapter of the book will include a personal plan that can be adapted for your own areas of development. This will work to keep you supported, empowered and on track.

Bring it on!

PART 1

What's it all about?

CHAPTER 1

What does being assertive really mean?

Be great in act, as you have been in thought.

William Shakespeare

A small boy in rags gets up from the table and, with enormous trepidation, he approaches the intimidating figure looming over the cauldron of gruel. Using every ounce of courage he says, with trembling anxiety, 'Please, sir, I want some more'.

This well-known scene from Charles Dickens' *Oliver Twist* is one of the most memorable moments in English literature and its message is loud and clear: speak your mind, particularly to one hierarchically above you (parent, employer, bank manager, etc.) and you risk being publicly humiliated and facing dire consequences. It can feel like a risk that may not pay off, and that is a huge thing indeed. The trepidation felt by Oliver in that critical moment is one we have all experienced and remember well from various times in our lives to date.

This fear can be so ingrained that we don't always realise it has become a fact in our heads. The idea that speaking up equals negative feelings and consequences has buried itself deeply in our subconscious and the thought can be ever-present, lurking deep in our minds.

And the intimidation that keeps this concept company can be debilitating because we start to believe that if we speak up there will be some sort of earth-shattering consequence to our actions. There are many examples that validate the 'truth' of this idea in the world at large, so why would we challenge it?

Of course, if you think about it there are just as many significant examples that disprove this 'truth', but our brains are very practised at ignoring things that do not reinforce our view of the world. After all, isn't the bad stuff easier to believe? Especially having been exposed in childhood to a range of examples of it being a risky thing to stand up for yourself against authority, via personal experience, stories, books and films. These factors come together to make it pretty much inevitable that the fears become deeply established by the time we reach adulthood.

All of which makes it easy to see why both children and adults feel uneasy about being assertive and honest. We are all battling against a deeply rooted fear that we will be punished, rejected or humiliated, viewed as an idiot, labelled a failure, or at the very least be seen as 'a bit odd' if we dare to state how we really feel. So why would we take the risk? Much better to play it safe and keep our heads down.

Now this is the bit where you get curious. Is that really true? Undoubtedly it can be a tough call to make, especially in the heat of the moment. It can feel risky and unsafe, and for most of us it can be far easier if we don't venture into that territory. It is far simpler to push things onto the bottom of the pile and 'forget' to deal with them.

But there are consequences to that sort of behaviour too. Ones that are far less desirable or productive than standing up for what is really right for us and risking what might follow. After all, if we don't go there then we will never really know.

brilliant example

When I was five years old, and in my first year of school, I remember feeling suddenly desperate for the loo. I did not want to shout out for fear of being told off by the classroom assistant, Mrs Anderson, for not raising my hand first (my hand had been raised for what seemed like an age and nobody had noticed), and there was a huge queue for book marking happening by the desk of the teacher, Mrs Chapman. So instead of pushing to the front to ask permission to go to the toilet, or even just leaving the classroom to go, I waited obediently in line. It took forever and yes, you guessed it, I ended up having a rather humiliating accident on the wooden floor. So my then lack of assertiveness for fear of being told off or being seen as disobedient meant I ended up in a far more embarrassing situation in reality. Right in front of the blackboard too!

When we end up doing things we don't want to do or going along with things we don't agree with, and we don't speak up and say what we want to say, then it is a very big issue indeed. It is a big deal to be unassertive because it feels disempowering, frustrating and generally out of control, in a kind of implosive way. It can be lonely and miserable and we can feel very lost when we are stuck there with what feels like no options.

The flip side to this is that when we feel so disempowered or frustrated we may end up flying into overly-assertive or perceived 'aggressive' behaviour to try and make up for it. Unfortunately this has the same effect – it's out of control and disempowering and has the added disadvantage of upsetting other people. None of this is productive for our careers, none of this builds good relations and none of this equals success. And if we are out of control we can become untrustworthy, incapable. What's more, other people will see us as unable to cope and generally unreliable. Not a recipe for success.

A history of assertiveness

It is an interesting exercise to look briefly at what happened to some of those in history who dared to raise their heads above the parapet for things they strongly believed in. These people, however far back they might go historically, show us that if you actually do speak up and assert yourself then the human race either adores you or wants you publicly reprimanded. Often the facts as they are laid out in history would have us believe that there is no middle ground at all in life and that any action whatsoever will only result in one of two extreme responses – either love or hate. It is easy to forget that usually responses fall into neither of these categories and are, in fact, far more complex.

William Wallace, leader of the Wars for Scottish Independence

Wallace rallied Scotland to rise up against Edward I, winning battles against huge odds. He was hanged, drawn and quartered in 1305 at a young age for high treason. Opinion is divided as to whether he was a hero or a villain.

Elizabeth I, queen of England 1558–1603

A strong, highly-educated woman who ruled with a hand of steel in a world of men. Her reign was known as 'The Golden Age' and she died a much-loved and respected monarch.

Winston Churchill, British WWII prime minister

Despite an early career in which he was shouted down and ignored by his political peers, Churchill was tenacious in refusing to accept defeat by Nazi Germany and led Britain to victory in World War II. He died a national hero.

Che Guevara, freedom fighter in Cuba and South America

Perceived as a rebel and a saviour of men, Guevara stood up against economic inequalities, resulting in a successful revolution in Cuba. He was executed by the CIA-assisted Bolivian forces in 1967.

Margaret Thatcher, prime minister of Britain 1979–90

Thatcher was adored and despised in equal measure by the

public for her extreme measures in what she saw as a solution to the economic crisis of the 1970s. She never waivered in what she believed to be the right course.

Florence Nightingale, nurse 1844–1910

Born into a rich, upper-class family, Nightingale turned her back on the then-traditional role of women, that of being a wife and mother, to educate herself as a nurse in order to serve the wounded in the Crimean War. She shunned several proposals of marriage in favour of committing to her career. On her return she fought the establishment for improvements to nursing, which benefit us to this day.

Whether you agree with these people's viewpoints or not, and whatever you think about them on the whole, there is no denying that the list consists of those who have been clear with their boundaries and have handled some potentially tricky situations in strong, measured and assertive ways in order to move things forward.

It is the negative perceptions that surround them (selfish, rude, ruthless and dangerous, among others) that can make us think it is not such a good idea to be assertive, and the more positive perceptions (brave, honest, strong, ambitious, forward-thinking) that make us aspire to be more like these key figures.

What are the benefits of being assertive?

The most famous benefit of being assertive is the ability to say no, or at least not to say yes so quickly and therefore end up biting off more than you can chew. But there are other benefits:

- The confidence to get your voice heard in any situation, be it one-to-one or in large meetings.
- Having the clarity to say exactly what you want and to have people hear it.

- The capacity to better manage conflict and confrontations.
- Having more options around what to say or do, rather than feeling disempowered by the lack of choice in the heat of the moment.

What a lack of assertiveness can cost us

When you lack assertiveness things can become quite unpleasant:

- We can end up feeling very stuck in situations where we are not happy or comfortable.
- We feel afraid of the consequences if we dare to state how we feel.
- We end up taking on too much through saying yes too easily, and then we get angry.
- We make do with disrespectful behaviour, bad service, bad food or faulty goods because we don't want to cause a fuss or create conflict.

This can all lead to us feeling very low and disempowered and can be incredibly damaging to our confidence levels. We also end up being afraid and possibly resentful of people in authority or in senior positions. We stop looking at them as simply another human being and allow their title to intimidate us. We are terrified of being criticised and not being liked.

When we have a lack of assertiveness it tends to be an indication of low self-esteem. Through not speaking up about what we think or feel we end up giving ourselves a hard time and feeling worse. Eventually this can become incredibly stressful and can sometimes be the root of anxiety and depression-related illnesses.

What gets in the way of being assertive?

We are all aware of what assertive and effective communication looks like but it can be quite a different matter when it comes to actually doing it. Many things can get in the way: a lack of confidence in the ability to be able to communicate well; the fear of not being liked or approved of; not being seen to be helpful; or the worry that you might lose your job if you don't say yes or help out by doing that little bit of extra overtime. Sometimes a fear of being perceived as too weak or easily taken advantage of can lead to overly-assertive behaviour, which can damage relationships just as much as the under-assertive behaviour.

Most of the time these fears that reside deeply in our subconscious are unfounded and bear no resemblance to what the likely outcome will be. Our brains tend to go to the worst-case scenarios and expect that they will happen if we go anywhere remotely near any assertive behaviour. In actual fact, as we've discussed, those fears are very inaccurate. Why would someone be that cross when we are simply asking for what we want?

More importantly, it is key that we remember that we are not the centre of everyone else's universe – only our own. By which I mean, we can think that other people find our comment or request a big deal because we find it a big deal in our heads. In actual fact, we have just a small impact on anyone else's day. You know all of the stuff you have to manage and juggle on any average day? Well, guess what – everyone else has the same amount of stuff too. We all have far more important things to be worrying about than the odd exchange over a piece of work or piece of overtime. Keeping things in perspective is highly important.

It is imperative that we always have in mind the idea that we experience ourselves from an internal perspective (our thoughts and feelings) and yet we experience other people from an external one (how they are behaving and what they say). We then judge ourselves comparatively, which can affect our self-confidence. For other people it is the other way around. This can be a tricky equation to balance in life.

It is rare that we ever come across to others exactly as we think we are coming across. More often than not it is the strong internal fears we have around 'being too strong' or 'not being pushed around' that can give us a false indication of how we are being perceived, and therefore means we hold back or give out more than we need to. In order to get a gauge for how your behaviour is representing your internal state, try the exercise below.

brilliant exercise

1   Write a list of things that you feel have annoyed, upset or frustrated you, either in the past or you might use some current examples:

_____

_____

2   Write down your feelings about the situations:

_____

_____

3   What were/are your thoughts about what happened?

_____

_____

4   Now list any of the behaviours associated with the thoughts and feelings above.

_____

_____

5   Does/did any of the above truly communicate what you wanted to communicate to the other people involved? Does/did the behaviour represent your thoughts or feelings?

_____

_____

It is important to remember that other people are not mind-readers, and though it might be crystal clear to us how things are landing, unless we are able to indicate this to others through our external behaviour, they may not be aware.

So, for example, imagine your manager has asked you to stay late again to make changes to that report for the umpteenth time – do you feel taken advantage of and as if you are delivering way above your job spec? Have you found a way to indicate this to your boss? If not, how is she/he supposed to know? You can't presume that your definition of unreasonable behaviour is the same as theirs.

It's so important to let people know when you are unhappy with their behaviour. It gives them the chance to do something about it. Usually it doesn't take much of a shift for people to realise they have overstepped some sort of boundary. So instead of festering and sulking about it, find a way to address the problem and offer your boss some solutions that will help you both.

brilliant example

Sam said that he thought Lars was doing too much at work and looked terrible as a result. Lars felt insulted, firstly because he felt he was responsible enough to gauge whether or not he was doing too much and, secondly, he thought it was downright rude of Sam to comment on his appearance like that. Lars responded with, 'Do you?' At which point Sam replied, 'Buddy, have you looked in the mirror?' Lars then felt even more patronised and insulted but felt there was nothing else he could say. The whole day Lars carried feelings of resentment that affected his working relationship with Sam for quite a while afterwards.

Does the behaviour do justice to the internal thoughts and feelings of Lars? Sam had no idea he was annoying Lars, and in his mind believed he was being helpful and supportive in showing that he had noticed how much Lars was working and that he was actually genuinely concerned.

▶

How else might Lars have managed the situation? What else could he have said? There is no one 'right' way to manage this situation of course, but there are a range of options. Even if Lars had chosen simply to say nothing it would have had a different effect. Sam would have known that Lars had a handle on things, or at least did not appreciate his intervention. Or Lars may have said something simple like, 'I'm aware of my workload and I'm actually okay with it.' The point is, the answer needs to be something that Lars is comfortable with, something that serves his purpose and, in this case, also takes care of Sam's concern to some extent.

Think about any situations where you have been in a similar position, i.e. on the receiving end of criticism or concern. Write some of them down and then see if you might have liked to have said or done something different in response. Then imagine that is what you did do. Imagine you said or did that ideal response. Notice how you feel when you imagine it. You could feel like this all the time in life when you start to operate from a more assertive position. It is more empowering and it is more productive.

> If you do what you've always done, you'll get what you've always got.
>
> Mark Twain

Degrees of assertiveness

Often people tend to refer to assertiveness as aggressiveness, and the opposite is often referred to as quiet or reserved. So, if aggressiveness sits at level 10 on a spectrum and forthrightness sits at level 8, then it could be said that quietness sits across 1, 2 and 3. If this is the case then it makes sense that assertiveness would sit across levels 4, 5, 6 and 7, in a flexible mid-ground.

This means, then, that if you are naturally quite reserved and speaking up does not come easily, assertiveness is just as accessible to you by aiming for level 4 or 5, which is not a huge stretch, as it is to those of you who may be naturally strong and direct on the spectrum (who would be aiming at around level 7).

If assertiveness were a see-saw, we'd like it balancing in varying degrees at all times. Ideally we don't want either side to hit the ground.

1	2	3	4	5	6	7	8	9	10

Reserved, not wanting to offend   Assertiveness   Forthright, strong   Aggressive

The assertiveness spectrum

Within this middle ground of assertiveness are a massive range of options that we will further explore in Part 2. For now, just begin to consider your options and get your brain used to the concept of consciously choosing how you want to respond.

Good assertiveness

brilliant example

'We're going to need to you to stay on for another hour this evening' was a statement often made by Ben's boss. And Ben's reply was often the same: 'Sure, okay, I think I can do that.' This happened for several weeks when Ben was new in his job at a media company.

When it got to month three Ben started feeling taken advantage of so he went back through his diary and added up the extra hours he had done. It came to 25 in total, which was the equivalent of three extra days' pay (around £500). The next time his boss asked him to stay he said he couldn't at such short notice this time, and then arranged to meet with his boss the next day.

At the meeting Ben calmly asked what the arrangement regarding those extra 25 hours was and he was told that it was 'just expected.' Ben asked to have his contract reviewed by saying: 'I completely understand that workload is heavy at the moment and I am more than happy to do my share. I wonder if we could review my contract so that I could accommodate these extra hours more willingly and ensure that I know ahead of time so that I can give the job my all.'

What was important about Ben's request was that he asked to have the review process in calm, neutral language and in a fair manner. So it would have been pretty strange for anyone to think that this was a weird or unfair request. And, more to the point, the situation got resolved very quickly, meaning that Ben did not feel resentful any longer about the extra time he was working because it had been agreed by contract and the boundaries were much clearer from both points of view.

brilliant example

Gemma worked at a reception desk at a big university and regularly had paperwork 'dropped' on her desk. She had got into the habit of just picking up the paperwork (which normally had a Post-it note on the front telling her what to do) without question and doing exactly as was requested as soon as she could. But that was getting stressful and her own workload was suffering significantly.

After a conversation with a newly recruited colleague, Gemma realised that these expectations were a result of what she had unconsciously made the norm. By always making it okay for people to 'dump' their papers on her desk, and always doing the work in record time, she had been largely responsible for setting that pattern of work. She realised that she had to break it.

The next time someone put papers on her desk, Gemma stood up and calmly called after them, using their name:

G: 'Shane?'

S: 'Yeah.'

G: 'What are these papers?'

S: 'Well if you read the Post-it …'

G: 'Actually Shane, could *you* fill me in?'

S: 'Erm … they are for the meeting tomorrow.'

G: 'Don't you have the time to do them?'

S: 'Well I'm really busy.'

G: 'I'm really busy too I'm afraid.'

By using his name in a level manner and asking questions, Gemma helped Shane realise that he couldn't just dump stuff on her desk and expect it to be done in the wink of an eye.

She was not being confrontational, after all Shane probably wasn't deliberately taking advantage of her, he was just doing what everyone did and was probably completely unaware of the impact of his behaviour. All Gemma had to do was reset the communications and expectations so her colleagues would have more awareness next time around. And, in this instance, she did it incredibly well.

Observe how other people handle tricky situations around needing to create some pushback, and acknowledge these responses for yourself. Whether you think it is a fitting response or not, note the reasons why you think what you do. By unpicking situations for ourselves, and being specific about what works and what doesn't, we can start to look more closely at the components within assertiveness that will allow us to come across more effectively in tricky situations.

brilliant recap

- Assertive behaviour is on a spectrum and not one fixed thing
- Our awkwardness around being perceived as assertive or unassertive often stems from conditioned behaviour in childhood
- Public perception of assertive role models tends to differ depending on the individual
- We often imagine that our response to a person or situation will be more harsh than it is likely to be in actuality
- Assertiveness is not the same thing as being aggressive or forthright and sits in a far more flexible and accessible middle ground

CHAPTER 2

Why we do too much for people

We fear doing too little when we should do more. Then atone by doing too much, when perhaps we should do less.

Robert Trout, news reporter

*D*espite our knowing on an intellectual level that we need to be more assertive, it seems that every one of us has experiences of doing too much for people and then becoming angry or frustrated because of the consequences. So what is it that causes us to do this and how can we start to take charge of it all more effectively?

But I like to help out

It feels really good to do things for other people. It's charitable and generous and friendly and supportive and all other things that can make life a much nicer place to be. And, if we're honest, it is quite nice when people go above and beyond for us – it makes us feel loved and special.

For these reasons, among many others, we do good things and often go over and above the call of duty and can end up taking on way too much. Generally we like to be loyal and true to our own values, usually because they are a strong part of our identity, but if we are not careful we can end up putting someone else's values, priorities or workload above the importance of our own and doing way too much as a result.

For example, you may not think it is right to see someone struggling with something that you could help them with straightforwardly enough and make their lives much easier – this might be helping a person at the train station carry a pushchair up the stairs or it might be helping someone at work to suss out how to solve a problem for which you can clearly see the solution. These things are fine until you become the go-to person all of the time and end up putting your own things at the bottom of the priority pile, and having your time invaded to the point where you end up working all sorts of ridiculous hours to make up for the time you spent helping someone else.

If you end up pushing your own tasks down in order to serve someone else then all too quickly you can end up doing way too much and feeling pretty resentful about it. This can cause those over-assertive explosions, such as tears or anger, because we cannot understand why the other person can't see that they are pushing a button in us.

But why would they? They can only see our external behaviour as an indication and usually that involves smiling, nodding or other placating behaviour. Then, when we explode it comes over as irrational, unpredictable and 'out-of-the-blue', when actually it has been brewing within you for ages. But saying 'no' can feel just too unhelpful. So instead we tend to default to the 'yes' word.

Saying yes

Fundamentally, saying yes to someone is positive. It is a great relief to hear the word 'yes' as a response when you're asking for some much-needed help. It generates a warm glow for the person doing the relieving because they are creating support for someone else. This is all fantastic stuff.

Saying yes helps to build and maintain professional and personal relationships. It is sympathetic to others who may be new to a situation, overloaded, going through a tough time due to all sorts of possible reasons, or may just need a second opinion or some alternative thoughts.

There are many reasons why we do helpful things for people. We might have had a similar experience 'back in the day' and feel that we can shed some light for them in order to help them move forwards. Or we can offer understanding to someone going through a situation that resonates with our own personal experiences.

So what's the difference between not doing enough, doing what is appropriate and doing too much? It's all about how we experience it internally, and these feelings can often be quite buried or subtle.

We forget that there are other choices around what we say or do. Our brain tends to trick us into thinking that if we don't say yes then we have to say no. We forget that there is compromise, or that we could partly help out. We forget that if it feels like someone is taking advantage there are options other than saying nothing or saying everything in a big out-of-control explosion. We could have a conversation about things, we could use humour, and all sorts of other options to address the issue without creating conflict.

Doing what is appropriate

- Is enjoyable.
- Doesn't take time or effort away from your own priorities and needs.
- Is born out of a genuine want to help without putting yourself at the bottom of the pile.
- Is conditional.
- Feels fair and just.
- Is a new option to be explored.

Add some more words of your own to help you start to do what is appropriate, instead of the yes/no extreme choices:

_____

_____

Doing too much

● Isn't enjoyable.

● Takes time or effort away from your own priorities and needs.

● Is born out of a thought around what you think you 'should' do rather than want to do.

● Feels unfair, there is an awareness of what you are not getting back by giving.

● Feels unjust and often breeds resentment.

Add some more of your own thoughts or feelings about when you do too much for people:

_____

_____

 Half of the troubles of this life can be traced to saying yes too quickly and not saying no soon enough.

Josh Billings, American humorist

brilliant exercise

1   Take the time to think about a situation where you are currently doing or giving a lot for/to somebody. Outline it below:

_____

_____

2   Consider all of the benefits to that person. Make a list:

_____

_____

3   Now think about if there are any drawbacks by giving too
    much to them. Again, you may find it useful to write these
    down:

_____

_____

4   Weigh up the pros and cons for this particular situation:

Pros	*Cons*
_____	_____
_____	_____
_____	_____
_____	_____
_____	_____

5   Now what about you? What would be the benefits for you if
    you were to push back a little and not say yes so quickly in this
    situation?

_____

_____

6   Would there be any drawbacks for you if you pushed back?

_____

_____

7   Consider what you are being given back in this situation:

_____

_____

▶

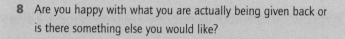

8 Are you happy with what you are actually being given back or is there something else you would like?

_____

_____

9 How could you manage the situation for yourself? What might you say or do that accommodates you best? (This might be saying you can't help at all, or it may be that you still do help but vocally express what you have going on too, and that you can only spend x amount of time helping them.)

_____

_____

By thinking about the above, you are likely to be starting to get a raised awareness about how you are really feeling concerning certain situations or behaviours. You may also be starting to get an insight into whether or not your responses are really communicating what you'd like them to, in order to keep yourself happier and treated with the respect you deserve.

Using your growing self-awareness

Once you become more aware of your own habits, it's important to notice how you respond to different people and situations. Many of us have a tendency to give ourselves a hard time if we realise we haven't done or said the thing we would have liked to have done or said. Don't do this. Put down the metaphorical stick with which you are beating yourself. Life is hard enough!

Put more positively, think of it as gaining further self-awareness so that you can move forward with a stronger, firmer and more confident stride. Remember that starting to become more assertive doesn't happen overnight and it needs to occur in tiny shifts, even if those shifts are simply a change of perception. A change of perception is still a good shift. Metaphorically pat yourself on the back instead of using that stick.

brilliant example

Rachel felt she was somehow giving too much to her boyfriend. She couldn't put her finger on quite what it was, but she felt unsettled most of the time and seemed to get unreasonably upset in the relationship if he rescheduled or changed plans at the last minute.

She made a list of all of the reasons why she 'gave' in the relationship, be it making a meal or simply listening and trying to be supportive when he moaned about his work situation, his friends or his family. It was part of the recipe for a good relationship wasn't it? And she'd want him to do the same for her.

She really wanted this relationship to work. She wanted to please him and have him think she was the best girlfriend he could possibly have. And being supportive and unselfishly loving made her feel good about herself.

Then she considered the drawbacks: he expected more and more from her, but at the same time he let her down more and more. He didn't realise that this 'giving' took effort from Rachel, he just presumed that it was his due, and if she pushed back he thought it odd.

She also realised that by constantly behaving in this manner she was standing in the way of him moving forward with his own life, his own relationships with others and his own realisations because she constantly picked up the responsibility for things going well and not going well. And the pattern became that he blamed her for these too. Quite an imbalance in responsibility and energy!

Rachel was unintentionally putting unrealistically sustainable behaviours into the relationship. Not only that, she resented playing what seemed like a mother role and felt she was being taken advantage of as he took more and more of her energy and gave less and less of his respect.

Rachel then started giving herself a hard time about the relationship and blamed herself for things not going as well as they could have, because she now believed her lack of assertiveness was to blame.

What needed to happen was a shift in behaviour. The problem was that this shift in behaviour might have meant the end of the relationship because Rachel's boundaries would have had to become stronger. This was Rachel's strongest fear. However, through not taking care of herself first and foremost in the relationship, the destructive domino effect on her was huge.

What's actually going on?

The example above is a common one in relationships. One partner can often feel they are giving too much and the other taking too much. The fear might be around losing the partnership and being alone. Or it might be something else completely.

What is at the core is that the person who often plays the 'giving' role is prioritising someone else over themselves, which, in the long term, tends to lead to resentment. And this resentment will always come out at some stage.

The same is true in any business relationship. And of course the fears around that can be even greater: loss of job and therefore income, particularly in times of economic downturn; not getting on with people at work; or not creating opportunities for career growth or promotion. Often this comes at the expense of health if it goes on too long – stress, illness, injury, depression, anxiety, substance dependencies. In these instances the work comes before the self and the destructive effects can be enormous.

By pushing ourselves down in importance on our own list of priorities, often without realising that we are even doing it, those small feelings of injustice or disagreement get pushed down too, and the more we take on the more buried they become.

Think of it like filling a sock drawer. The more socks you have to squeeze into the drawer in order to shut it, whatever the struggle, the more likely the sock drawer is to give way (either the bottom falls out, or the sides or front come apart, or the drawer gets jammed – hopefully this is not just my sock drawer?!).

Human beings are really not much different. Feelings can only get pushed down for so long before they resurface or push back. Feelings and thoughts have to be acknowledged somehow before it gets to explosion point and they fly out uncontrollably because we can't hold them in any more. Our emotional drawer is way too full.

What is it that is really going on then, to make us put ourselves bottom of our own lists? To make ourselves pack down our negative feelings, which happen to let us know that all is not well? It is probably fair to say that people are rarely very conscious of doing it, but long-term patterns can root themselves deep and can quickly have us and others believe that our behaviour and habits are 'just the way we are', or that it's 'just in our nature.'

In fact, neither of those things ring true, and you do have a choice to behave differently in order to be more in charge and not so taken advantage of. But this unknown landscape of choice can be scary territory to venture into when we haven't been aware of it before.

> I've realised that being happy is a choice. You never want to rub anybody up the wrong way or not be fun to be around, but you have to be happy. When I get logical and I don't trust my instincts – that's when I get in trouble.

Angelina Jolie, actress

Thought statements

brilliant exercise

Check the list below and tick the thought statements that apply to you:

I want everything to go perfectly.

I want to be a success story.

If I don't do it then nobody else will.

I've 'messed up' in the past and don't want to do it again so I make a conscious effort to do things right.

I worry about being rejected.

I like being popular.

I feel good when I receive praise and compliments for my achievements (and I get hurt or angry when I don't).

I treat others as I would like to be treated.

It feels good to impress people with what I can do well.

I want people to talk about me and my achievements.

Add any other thought statements that you are aware go through your mind:

_____

_____

_____

_____

Challenging thought patterns

By becoming aware of our own internal thought patterns then we can begin to tackle the internal resistance we have around being assertive, which may not be serving us so well.

Take each thought and challenge how true it is on a percentage scale. For example:

'If I don't do it then nobody else will.' How true does this feel?

Initially this might feel like it is 99 per cent true but is it really?

'Well, someone else might do it … if they had to. But they are used to me doing it. And anyway I like doing it.' Aha!

So now we are in the realms of choice. You can choose to do something because you like doing it or you can choose not to because you don't want to or you would like someone else to do it for once. Either way, there is still a shift from how it feels to say to yourself 'If I don't do it nobody else will' to saying 'I enjoy doing it so I'd like to do it' or 'I know I usually do this, but this time I would like someone else to do it.'

After considering these options, how true on a percentage scale does that original statement feel? About 55 per cent? Less? The presence of choice has an amazing effect on we human beings, particularly when we start to recognise how much choice we have in everything we do and say.

brilliant tip

If you are faced with a question or a difficult situation, where possible buy yourself time so as to break the pattern of your usual response. Start to use expressions like, 'Let me get back to you shortly', 'Give me two minutes' and 'I will be right with you', just to allow yourself the headspace to weigh things up in your mind and consider your options before you give your response on the assertive spectrum.

Just remember that it is completely fine to do things for people, so long as you genuinely want to do them. If there are any begrudging feelings raising their little heads then pay attention to what these are about sooner rather than later. Learn to listen to what your instincts are saying to you. Once you have some clarity about what is really going on for you then you can find an appropriate way to communicate your feelings to people, or find a slightly different way of responding behaviourally.

 **brilliant** recap

- The next time someone asks you to do something, notice how quickly you might say yes, or indeed how difficult it is to say no

- Consider other options you may have, other than saying yes or no

- What else might you be able to say instead that still feels okay for you but lets the other person know that you are going above the call of duty for them?

- Is there anything else you could say around not helping, or doing less than usual?

- Take note of your thought patterns and challenge if they really are fact, or if you have unconsciously limited your own thinking around the possible outcomes of a situation or relationship

CHAPTER 3

What we're told to do

An appeaser is one who feeds a crocodile – hoping it will eat him last.

Winston Churchill, British politician

Very often we say yes because we think we should. These 'shoulds' are frequently the keys to shifting our behaviours. They come from the rules we are exposed to from birth until now and are often strongest from what we have been told to do during our upbringing, education and in the earlier stages of our professional lives.

None of us was born with these rules in our heads. We learned them from others and put them together from our own life experiences to date. Some of them serve us well and others less so. Some used to work and we have now moved on from them or outgrown them. For the most part, though, rules do keep us stuck if we don't stay conscious of them and question them regularly.

The great thing about this is that if we can learn things that aren't serving us well, we can also unlearn them. But first we need to work out what 'they' are. So let's have a look at the various life stages and experiences in our lives and start to piece together where our own set of rules might come from.

Babyhood

Throughout history there have been all sorts of 'rules' about bringing up babies and getting them into routines. And that advice has been conflicting. Different people believe different things.

Some believe it is good to get babies 'into a routine' early, which is often the only practical way to go, especially for the modern parent. Babies learn very quickly when they 'should' or 'should not' make too much noise, for example. Others believe that the baby will 'tell' you what it wants and when. Babies in these circumstances may well learn that they get what they need whenever they behave in a particular way.

However, leaving small babies to cry for any length of time beyond a few minutes has now been proven to have a strong impact on their personal development and feelings of security as both child and adult. The lack of personal touch for a baby can result in the same feelings as those directly linked to lower levels of security and therefore affects the confidence that allows assertiveness in adulthood.

If a small baby is taught that they 'shouldn't cry', even when it is their only means of communicating something, then they start to distrust their own instincts and have stronger anxieties as they grow up. As people get older these can manifest as either over-assertiveness or under-assertiveness in order to try and rebalance what they need with how they feel.

Because these behavioural habits begin way back in babyhood, it can become very difficult to recognise them in adulthood – they are so deeply rooted that it feels as though they are simply in our DNA. And when habits are that old and that deep, it can lead to feelings and thoughts that say things such as, 'nobody else seems to be like that', 'what is wrong with me?', 'why do I overreact?', 'I have no self-control!' and on and on and on.

The list of thoughts can be endless and the brain going round on loop like this can be a very unhelpful and unpleasant place to be in. If this place sounds familiar, then have some hope. It is very common indeed (in fact probably everyone has some degree of it at different times in their lives) and, most importantly of all, it can be shifted. Phew!

Toddling

We tend to get bombarded with many rules as toddlers. Cries of 'Don't touch', 'Be careful', 'Go with Daddy', 'Sit down nicely', 'Eat up' and so on can lead to us not knowing our bottoms from our elbows. Encouragement, or lack of it, coupled with these rules can result in feeling pressure and then so-called tantrums and tears before bedtime. In fact, most of the rules we hear as toddlers stay with us through our early adult lives, if not beyond.

For example, if toddlers aren't given the choice to not eat up if they don't want something then they grow up not trusting their own feelings or being aware of them at all, looking outside for rules rather than inside for signals. Eating is an interesting area as therein can develop a lot of other factors, but perhaps that's another book for another day. So, example number two then: if a toddler doesn't want to go with Aunty Maggie for whatever reason and they say so and are yet still made to go with her, then they are likely to start believing that that their voice is not being listened to and will either start pushing back or rebelling (over-assertive), or they won't say anything at all (under-assertive).

Of course, the reality is that there are all sorts of reasons around time and commitments why a child might be over-ridden ultimately, but engaging with them, whatever the circumstances, is essential. So if the child doesn't want to go with Aunty Maggie, then there are two main options: asking why not and seeing if a compromise can be reached with the child after hearing what they have said, or a simple acknowledgement that they have been heard and understood, are far more productive ways of moving forward.

Both of these options sit in the flexible middle ground of the assertiveness spectrum, where people listen to both sides and work out the best solution case by case. It sounds time-consuming and exhausting, but actually long-term it is far more time-economical.

And if we look at Eric Berne's Transactional Analysis model, a brilliant and simple model for all communication, then the answers are there.

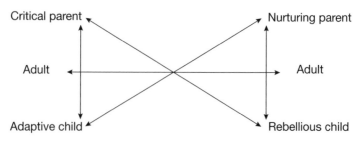

Eric Berne's Transactional Analysis Model

Berne's belief was that each person is made up of three *alter ego* states: parent, child and adult.

Parent state

Contains the authoritative voice that we think we 'should' have in order to be taken seriously and considered 'grown up' enough. This state tends to be influenced by external influences (i.e. imposed rules and belief systems).

Child state

Our real, internal reactions and feelings to people and situations tend to reveal our child state. When anger or despair dominates, our inner child is in charge. When we feel like we are on the back foot and our emotional needs take over, when we look to others to solve the situation for us, we tend also to be in child state.

Adult state

This is the ideal, and really encapsulates our ability to think and determine a course of action for ourselves, which we then execute with confidence. The adult in us keeps our parent and child states in an equilibrium that is far more useful in day-to-day communications.

If someone speaks to us like a nurturing parent ('That's a really good piece of work, well done', for example) or a critical parent ('What on earth are you doing with that client?') then we will respond as an adaptive child (usually behaviours around what is commonly referred to as people-pleasing – lots of smiling and trying to make things alright for everyone) or a rebellious child ('Stuff what they think, I'm going to do it anyway'), or we flit between the two states.

If we can gain the self-awareness to realise what is happening and regain the adult state then the other person has to respond as an adult – it's an essential balancing act and we need to be conscious of it. It's another version of the see-saw, which we can only balance if we know what is going on.

It's another way of looking at and identifying the flexible middle ground that serves us so well but yet we so often distrust. Due to its general lack of familiarity to us, it can feel like unsafe territory. The more we start to employ the adult-to-adult position, though, the more we notice how effective it is, despite the simplicity of the concept.

Pre-school

This is where a child's brain has to incorporate far more rules and instructions, which start to come from different people beyond parents and close friends/family. Here other children's parents start to come into the equation, as do teachers, carers and suchlike.

Think back to your own pre-school days. It is usually the time when, as a young child, you suddenly realise that not everybody lives life exactly like you do and that can be somewhat intriguing. Sometimes it can even feel scary or challenging. This new, wider world can make everything seem bigger and less convincing. In fact, the new rules introduced at nursery and playschool often help pre-schoolers to feel safe as they give the brain something to 'keep hold of.' Without the obvious presence of rules in any situation we often feel the need to look for them as a means to help us know where we're at, as a way of helping us not behave like we're 'mad' – one of the biggest fears of the human race.

Rules such as 'Sit on the mat for storytime', 'Line up for milk' and 'Put your paintings to dry safely in the corner' all help in creating the feelings of security and being looked after. They give structure and parameters. They are the beginnings of some of the 'rules of life' in terms of manners and getting along with others. They are the social conditioning, and the initial understanding that the presence of structure keeps some sort of order to things and protects people.

However, rules such as 'Put your hand up for permission to speak' and 'Put your fingers on your lips until everyone is quiet' aren't so helpful. They are one-sided rules where there is nothing in them for the child other than creating fear or anxiety. Again, it is better to operate from a fairer middle ground and make adjustments, such as 'the first person to put their hand up can speak first', which offers a reason and a benefit for the rule and is clearly defined. It isn't a rule that is there to simply prevent the adults from having to deal with chaos.

This flexible middle ground is preferable to operate in at all times. It will help children grow up understanding how to work within the fairer middle ground and with the confidence to communicate what is really going on for them, rather than being terrified of whether it is 'right' or whether they are 'allowed' to say things. Because this flexible middle ground is one that considers both sides, people tend to feel more comfortable voicing what they are feeling and a more honest communication will ensue as a result. This is far more productive in terms of moving undesirable situations forward.

A lack of awareness of the two or more sides of any situation – what's in it for them and what's in it for me – makes it very difficult for any person, whatever their age, to communicate openly and effectively. If we are only aware of one side or one perspective of any situation then the assertiveness balance disappears very quickly. Once gone it can be a tricky thing to reclaim because it becomes a difficult thing to see. It becomes invisible and falls off the radar and hence we feel stuck and frustrated yet again.

It is interesting that it is around this time in a child's pre-school development that they also start to build their own rules, put together by their own perceptions of the outside world. This is the time in a child's development where rules start to establish themselves that say things like, 'If I don't do as I'm told I won't be liked/loved', and there also starts to become a more heightened awareness of fitting in with others and an editing of behaviour in order to do so. Social conditioning kicks in hard and fast at this crucial stage of life.

Rules of the home

This is probably the trickiest to define since every household
is very different. The huge amount of variations of personality
can make up a range of at-home dynamics, but by breaking
down the main groups we can try to get more clarity on how
each individual's 'rules of the home' have affected and are still
affecting them.

Parents or guardians

Parents or guardians will put all sorts of rules in place for all
sorts of reasons. There are the rules about behaviour – what we
are or are not allowed to do, rules on playtime, teatime, bath-
time, bedtime, rules on how we talk to others, rules on keeping
things tidy, rules around the dinner table, rules on how to treat
siblings … Make a list of the parental/guardian rules you grew
up with that you remember:

_____

_____

_____

_____

_____

If you yourself are a parent/guardian this is a good opportunity to also explore the rules that you have set for the younger
members of your household. List them here and see if you can
identify where the rule comes from or why you think it is a good
rule to have. You may find that some serve both you and others
well. Or you may find that some could do with a rethink or a
scratch out. It is extremely important to note here that some
rules are productive, but the choice of which ones you choose to
live by is entirely yours.

Siblings, or no siblings

Eldest siblings tend to create rules for themselves very quickly about how they need to guide the way for any younger siblings, and how they are responsible for them to a certain degree. Along with these go some old classics, such as 'respect your elders.' Middle siblings are often told that they are the ones that 'fall under the radar', 'are the forgotten ones', and other things like that. Younger ones have a tendency to be told that 'they can get away with anything' or 'they are the spoilt ones.'

While there can occasionally be some truth in these sayings, they can also be quite mythical and out-of-date beliefs. Yet told these often enough by adults, young children will start to believe them to be absolute truths, which can be damaging.

An older sibling who believes they must lead the way will tend to be quite hard on themselves when they don't succeed at something and confidence can fall. Or they may rebel. Middle siblings can believe they aren't noticed and so don't really matter, which can lead to both over- and under-assertive behaviours. Younger siblings tend to believe that, by getting away with anything, they need to push the boundary more in order to be noticed and can therefore end up being hard work for themselves and others as they scream out for their own identity. Like a middle child, they may feel they need to work hard to be noticed rather than 'just being allowed' to do what they want.

Meanwhile only children can sometimes feel that they are solely responsible for pleasing both parents, which is an impossible task and can lead to damaging inner conflict unless nurtured ideally by both parents while growing up. Unresolved issues here create a strong feeling of not being good enough and a destructive need to be accepted.

The sibling dynamic on the whole tends to swing between arguments and/or solidarity, throwing up all sorts of assertiveness issues along the way. That said, it can be a good training ground for the wider world, and a large number of siblings tend to be good at asserting themselves in order to claim their personal space and have their own identity acknowledged.

Older relatives and other visitors

This is an interesting category because along with older relatives and visitors often comes the old and out-dated belief systems. However, these are the rules that we're regularly told not to question and to simply respect as children, even when they make no sense.

It's a tricky dilemma because you may want to explain to a child, 'Sweetheart, I know Great Aunty Helen thinks little girls should be seen and not heard, but she's quite old now and things are different to how they were when she was a child. Just go along with it for now so we can make it okay for Aunty Helen.' But the fear of that humiliating moment when the child utters, 'Aunty Helen, Mum thinks you're really old and out-of-date', can stop such a conversation from happening. This can, of course, lead to confusion and ultimately those family feuds from hell (of which we all have our own version – those screaming tantrums with door slams or those deathly silences for hours on end). Not good.

It is down to a lack of assertiveness itself when parents or guardians fail to stand up to their own beliefs in order not to offend or rock the boat with their visitors or older relatives. So, when a remark like, 'Don't question your elders', is put out into the room and the elders who normally accept being questioned say nothing to defend their usual position, it can send out very mixed messages to children. With the question, 'Can I speak up or not?', going round in their heads as well as, 'Be polite to the guests, darling', it doesn't take long for things to get squashed down internally only to burst out a bit later, from under-assertive to over-assertive in seconds. No middle ground. No spectrum in sight. It can mean that those 'bottoms on the see-saw' are being flung from one extreme to the other. And if the same thing happens regularly enough then the pattern very quickly gets set and the triggers need not be very much at all in the end.

Festivities

It's typical for extreme responses to happen around Christmas, or other similar festivals, when our levels of assertiveness tend to get tested way more than at other times of the year.

---

brilliant example

A few years ago, I excitedly packed up my bags to go and spend Christmas with a good friend of mine. It was great to have a change from the norm and I was really looking forward to helping her with the Christmas dinner I'd promised to get involved with. I love making the turkey moist and delicious and getting the cinnamon stick into the pan of cranberry sauce. To top it all, I love throwing glittery stuff over table cloths and making things look all swanky and my friend hates all that. Sam much prefers to honey-glaze parsnips, pour out the port and dance around to Wham's 'Last Christmas.'

Christmas morning started like a dream: giggles, presents, mini chocolates and a large coffee on the go, as well as a cheeky glass of champagne to kick off the day. With just the four of us (Sam and her husband, me and my boyfriend) I set massive expectations in my mind that the day was going to be utterly amazing. In fact it was going to be the best Christmas I had ever had.

Sam and I both glittered the table, placed the special cutlery and started the dinner preparations. I buttered and basted the turkey and got it into the oven, the timings all worked out to a tee. So far, so good … On went the Christmas CD and as Slade belted out I ran upstairs to put on my party frock and make-up before the guests arrived. And they did − early! I ran downstairs half-dressed anyway, we chinked our champagne glasses and off I flitted, still with wet hair, into the kitchen to baste the turkey again … ▶

and wash the sprouts … and put some more champagne in the fridge. And there I stayed, unintentionally.

My then-boyfriend kept sticking his head into the kitchen. 'Are you okay?', he would tentatively ask. 'Fine', I kept grinning (so convincingly), and danced around the kitchen in bare feet while drinking more champagne just to prove my point. My hair by this stage was starting to become a frizzy, wavy mop, having been 'naturally dried' by the heat of the cooker and pans. Not quite the slinky look I had envisaged when I packed my straighteners, hair serum and glitzy Christmas Day slides. Nor was planned the smell of sprouts, which had absorbed into my nice new Karen Millen top (grr!). Oh well …

'Well done you!', people kept shouting into the kitchen before they flitted back into the lounge for more chat and laughter.

Three hours later, three nails had snapped, my make-up had run and I looked a bit rough, to say the least. I was hot, heady and irritable. The dinner was done on time though and it did look amazing, even if I do say so myself. I had, of course, made up for my time of being trapped in the kitchen by helping myself to the champagne more regularly than I had intended. Oops.

Dinner was served and it was lovely – for them. I had to force down every mouthful, partly because I was sick of the sight of that dinner by the time I came to eat it and partly because I was so resentful that nobody had really helped me very much at all. But why would they? Every time they had popped their head in to see if they could help I had said, 'No, it's fine, really.' I had a plan to stick to and I didn't want them messing it up. And anyway, it would have taken ages to explain it all. It was far better to just do it myself, right?

By 5pm I had passed out on the sofa and was about as much fun as a pile of broken bricks. When I finally woke up ready to party everyone had either left or gone to bed and my boyfriend was snoring on the sofa opposite. Great! Merry Christmas! I consoled myself with bad Christmas television comedy specials and a box of Quality Street. The following morning I felt depressed and bloated and like I never wanted to see any one of them ever again. But whose fault was that really?

Deck the halls, jingle bells, presents, smiles, lovely meals and thank you very much, followed by tears, tantrums and off-you-go-to-bed-then. The festivities (be it weddings, Christmas, Yuletide, Hanukkah, Eid, Thanksgiving, or something else entirely) can always be relied upon to kick up the strongest emotions. And these tend to be a result of the strongest rules – usually the self-enforced ones. These rules tell us that families must get on at this time of year, that everything needs to be perfect, that everything must run like clockwork and that everyone needs to be suitably fed, impressed and made to feel welcome. In other words, there is no room for anything less than perfect, which means that there will always be disappointment. Human nature does not facilitate perfection. When will we ever learn that one?

Festive occasions and celebrations are probably the times where under-assertiveness and over-assertiveness swing back and forth like a Newton's cradle (or said see-saw). When people annoy each other, or simply get in each other's physical space too much, then misbehaviour rears its head and feelings tend to get pushed away because people want everything to go well ... whatever the cost. But again, this can only be done so much and then, bang! We get explosions ... or indeed implosions, depending on the people in question.

And when behaviour becomes reactive and out of control we often give ourselves a hard time. We think we have failed and get on the merry-go-round of blame and guilt. Therein lies the roots of stress, anxiety, short-temperedness and illnesses such as chronic fatigue or indeed worse. In short, it really isn't good for us to get caught in this trap.

Primary school and the rules of the playground

This is the age when we really start to develop our value system, those things that are most important to our sense of well-being, and inform our sense of what is 'right' and what is 'wrong.' It's also when we are trained to fit in with the crowd and not do anything too unique that could make us stand out, otherwise we may be laughed at or criticised.

Sadly, this is also the time when most of us, if not all, have some bad memories of being picked on, teased, or bullied in the playground. It can be a shock after those early years of nurturing to be on the receiving end of such unfair behaviour. Most children aren't equipped to understand how to deal with it and so, all too often, this playground misconduct results in fights, private tears or withdrawn behaviour for fear of being judged for being bullied.

It's easy to see how this can result in a sense of uncertainty or even fear and a lack of confidence. It can also form the basis of any low self-esteem and distrust we experience throughout life, and, let's face it, everyone has moments of low self-esteem, self-doubt and suspicions about others' motives.

So you can see how important it is that children are taught how to be assertive; sadly the schools that recognise this are very few and far between.

And if only it were just the kids that have this effect, but it is of course other children's parents and teachers who can also be guilty of lowering self-esteem. Parents who have an opinion on the child, rather than letting them be who they are. Remarks such as, 'Ooh, you're tall for your age', 'You really ought to eat less pudding', 'You're shy, aren't you?' and other thoughtless comments can impact on a child's self-esteem hugely when they are at primary school because they are made to feel 'different', when all they want to do is fit in.

The lines can also be blurred when teachers refer to certain behaviours with things such as, 'You're a very silly boy.' This puts the emphasis on the child, rather than the behaviour. But 'silly' behaviour isn't part of the boy's genetic make-up, it's simply something silly they did, probably through not thinking. How much better to say 'That was a silly thing to do', or even better, 'That wasn't a very sensible choice you made was it?' These admonitions criticise the behaviour and allow the child to learn from their mistake and recognise that they have the ability to make better decisions in the future.

This is a simple example, below, but shows just how easy it is for an unthinking adult to label children 'silly' or 'stupid' or 'good', and these labels can stick for a very long time.

brilliant example

Sally was the middle child of three. When she was a little girl her father discovered her crying. When he asked her why, she sniffed and said she thought she was stupid and ugly.

He took her in his arms and, from every good intention, said: 'My darling, you may not be as beautiful as your sister or as clever as your brother but you have the most important thing of all and do you know what that is?' Thrilled, she said, 'No, what?' He replied, 'You have been blessed with kindness and good sense.'

Until her middle-thirties Sally prided herself on these skills of being kind and sensible, but also truly believed that she possessed neither intelligence or looks (both not true). Her self-esteem at work was very high as she was extremely good at her job, organised and well-regarded by her colleagues as the sensible person who could be relied upon and was good to work with.

However, in her personal life she struggled to find love and always felt that she lacked the intelligence to be really good company. Her work organised for some coaching and it was only then that this deep-rooted belief was uncovered, and when it was challenged she realised that, while she was undoubtedly very 'kind and sensible', she was also intelligent and, in her own way, beautiful. Ten years on she is happily married with two small children.

It's powerful stuff!

Secondary school and the teenage years

So now we are entering what was likely to be the trickiest age bracket of them all. Here not only did we learn about protons, neutrons and the whys and wherefores of the French Revolution, but secondary school was the training ground for life.

It's where most of us had our first kiss, had our hearts broken for the first time and really learned about relationships. This is where we learned to be cool or else suffer endlessly, or rebel and refuse to fit into the norm, becoming resilient, independent and learning to deal with loneliness all at the same time. Whichever path we chose, we were on our personal quest to be respected and be noticed and when rules got in the way of doing either then they could feel like boulders in the road.

Rules in secondary school often seem harsh and unfair. Like no jewellery or designer labels, having to wear horrible navy-blue gym clothing or no make-up. 'But we're almost adults ... why not?!'

Even worse than in the younger days, many adults seem to fundamentally forget to talk to teenagers like human beings, and certainly not like adults.

Cast your mind back to those days and write down some of the adults you remember for negative reasons and why. For example, one female teacher at my secondary school once stopped me in the corridor to tell me that my skirt was way too short and looked terrible, particularly since I didn't have 'the slimmest legs in the world.' I was fourteen years old! You can imagine the years of impact on self-esteem that one had on me. I felt I was being spoken to as though I had no feelings whatsoever, and I was so angry and upset that I refused to return to school for the remainder of the day. In hindsight the comment was also incredibly sexist – would a boy have been told that he effectively looked unattractive because of his choice of outfit? What are your own examples, and how have they affected your self-esteem or belief systems in life?

_____

_____

_____

_____

_____

Now look at the positive examples from your life. For example, my German teacher, Mr Thomson, always listened to my point of view and engaged in conversation with me like an adult. He was very strict but only in terms of doing the work, taking responsibility for yourself and getting on in life. I really respected him and he always made me feel as though my thoughts and opinions were worth something. I think I have absorbed one or two of his values in my own adult years and always try to reinforce the value that everyone has something valuable to say.

Who features in your positive memories and why? What have you taken forward from them?

_____

_____

_____

_____

_____

Early working environment

Here assertiveness becomes an extremely tricky territory to explore because, after however many years we have spent in education, the rules change. Suddenly, not only is it a question of being accepted, it's an issue of keeping a job, beginning a career, impressing the right people and getting paid.

On many occasions I have heard people say that they take on jobs that they don't really want to do because they don't want to rock the boat, or they are scared of being made redundant in a challenging economic climate, or it will just be quicker if they do it themselves.

Ironically the fear of being too assertive and therefore not establishing boundaries (leaving work on time, taking the full lunch break, saying no to those extra pieces of work) can be the very thing that prevents progress at work. Showing confidence and strength of character, standing firm on boundaries and standing up for what you believe to be right are the key things that help people to get on at work.

So it seems there are some inconsistencies between school, college and work on these grounds.

 **exercise**

1   Make a list of some of the things you currently say yes to at work that you may not really want to do, or that are encroaching on your own time/energy in a negative way:

_____

_____

_____

_____

2   Now make a list of some of the things you actually say and do when accepting the pieces of work or responsibilities listed above:

_____

_____

_____

_____

3   List the things you would really like to say or do when these things are pushed your way:

_____

_____

_____

_____

▶

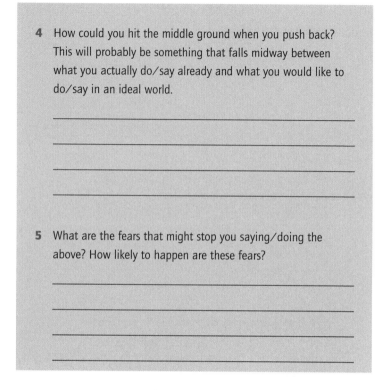

4   How could you hit the middle ground when you push back?
This will probably be something that falls midway between
what you actually do/say already and what you would like to
do/say in an ideal world.

_____

_____

_____

_____

5   What are the fears that might stop you saying/doing the
above? How likely to happen are these fears?

_____

_____

_____

_____

Adult relationships

This is one of the toughest dynamics we have to deal with in
terms of the rules and past experiences we often bring to them.
Battles, either overt or covert, about who is in charge, who has
control, not wanting to rock the boat, wanting things 'to work',
doing things for the sake of others (children, friends, etc.),
compromising and what all of that really means, can produce a
minefield of thoughts, feelings and behaviours. Because we are
emotionally entrenched in these personal relationships it can be
very tricky to get the objective viewpoints we need to change
things in order to positively create a move forward.

Indeed, it is fair to say that the way forward for any adult relationship is to allow people to be themselves and to provide

yourself with the inner support system you need, first and fore-most outside of the relationship. Easier said than done it is true. Hopefully the foundations addressed in this book can help to create the self-confidence needed to explore the range of options through choice and understanding.

 Is life not a hundred times too short that we should stifle ourselves.

Friedrich Nietzsche

Self-limiting beliefs

As human beings we are full of these – any of these sound familiar?

- 'I can't draw.'
- 'I'd never be able to do that.'
- 'I've got two left feet.'

Self-limiting beliefs are the thoughts hidden away in our sub-conscious, which say we can't do things. In other words, they are the excuses we make – and we've spent a lifetime constructing them.

Look out for phrases you either say out loud to others or in your head to yourself that include language such as, 'I've never been able to', or 'I simply can't', or 'I wish I could.' These are all indications of self-limiting beliefs taking place.

Often, with self-limiting beliefs we are unaware that they are going on because they are usually off the radar in terms of our consciousness. We repeat them to ourselves so much that they become solid and immovable road blocks to our very existence, which can really limit our quality of life and our happiness.

Sayings like, 'You can't have it all', are particularly strong cul-prits in helping to reinforce limitations that need not exist in our lives. Think about some of the things you take as fact in life and see if you can turn them into questions rather than statements.

Up until the age of six or seven years old Steve was a pretty good drawer and so were both of his siblings. Steve was the youngest child and his brother, who was just two and a half years older, was the strongest artist of the three of them, with particular strengths in steadiness and patience, which people would comment on regularly.

When Steve reached the age of eight he says he remembers telling himself that he wasn't the painter in the family and he decided he'd like his role to be something else because he didn't think both he and his brother could be arty and that they had to be different. When I asked him why he thought that he said that he believed it was because people regularly compared the brothers and it would be a way for them not to do that where art was concerned. It was a way for him to keep his feelings safe and not risk putting himself out there in case he was compared to his brother.

In other words, Steve failed to assert he was good at something and did not have the confidence to risk stating his ability in case he was put down. He had an irrational and unfounded fear about the consequences. Eventually he stopped drawing completely.

Last year, his mother was clearing out the cellar and he came across a pile of paintings and pictures done by children. He looked through them and said, 'Wow, Jamie was excellent even back then wasn't he?' 'They're yours love', replied his mother. Steve turned the pictures over and sure enough there was his name pencilled on the back from all those years before.

When we talk about asserting ourselves, and we are scared to in case x happens, we are in very similar territory. We tell ourselves we cannot do it, that other people are better at it than we are and that we simply have our strengths elsewhere in life. But that is not true. In doing this we are establishing self-limiting beliefs and creating a low ceiling for ourselves that can only ever end in feeling stifled, frustrated and stuck. The thing to remember is that because this 'ceiling' has been self-imposed we can also shift it if we choose to.

In the example above, the ceiling had been self-imposed for reasons that had become real in Steve's head but in actuality weren't true. This is an indication about how much we need to check the 'facts' as we tell them to ourselves and question if they are really true, or are they just what we tell ourselves in order not to step outside what we perceive as our comfort zone.

Dare to put pen to paper and you too might be a good drawer. Dare to assert yourself and you might just start to get the results that would be more productive for you. For some reason this can feel really very scary. So then, are we more scared of success than we are of failure? Is that why we aren't as assertive as we would like to be?

brilliant tip

Create a list of all of the things you believe you are <u>not</u> good at or even that you think you are incapable of. Now challenge that list. How true is it really?

Sometimes we have told ourselves that we can't do things, but actually it turns out we can and they might even be one of our neglected strengths. Encourage yourself to take responsibility for the way you have limited yourself so far in your life, and make a conscious decision to change that.

Challenging self-limiting beliefs

brilliant exercise

Get used to keeping a notebook or diary for a short period of time (a couple of weeks is a good length). Note down some of the exchanges you have had, from a basic exchange at a checkout counter to a more meaningful conversation with a close friend. Now take some time to think about how what was said affected you and think about how what you said affected the person you talked to. Start to deduce your own thoughts from these encounters and note where you would place some of these exchanges on the assertiveness scale.

This exercise helps to gain a more conscious awareness of your own patterns of behaviour and then to work out why you do what you do. Some things you may find are serving you well and, in these cases, that is a great feeling in itself. With other examples, you may find that you would like to respond differently.

A look at day-to-day rules
Write down your own list of the rules that go through your head every day. These might be things like, 'I should eat breakfast', 'I shouldn't drink too much caffeine', 'I shouldn't be late', 'I should get more done with my day', and so forth.

SHOULDS   *SHOULDN'TS*

_____   _____

_____   _____

_____   _____

_____   _____

_____   _____

_____   _____

When you read back through this list, notice if you recognise these rules as coming from others who have had influence in your life or whether they belong entirely to you.

Go back through your list with a pen or pencil and scratch out the 'should' and 'shouldn't' words and replace both with the word 'could', e.g. 'I could eat breakfast', 'I could drink too much caffeine', etc. What do you notice once you have done this and have re-read the list to yourself? Do you feel differently? Write down any observations below:

_____

_____

_____

_____

_____

_____

_____

This exercise is a good one to introduce the concept of choice, and for the human being to realise that choice is totally and utterly up to them. It's just a matter of going for what is appropriate in any given situation or context. You have the ownership and responsibility to decide that for yourself.

brilliant recap

- We learn the rules whereby we live our day-to-day lives, whether through others or through our own experiences

- Our childhood experiences can have a significant effect on whether or not we have the self-esteem to exist in the flexible middle ground of assertiveness

- Not all rules are bad, it is simply worth questioning for ourselves why they are there

- We have the choice as to whether or not we decide to follow our own rules or whether we decide to challenge/change them

- We are responsible for the development of our own self-limiting beliefs

Once we start to strip away some of these rules and we start to look at the whys and wherefores of how they came about, then we can start to identify who we actually are at our core. We can start to look at what really does make us tick – for example, what makes us irritated and what makes us happy. We can start to see who we really are as individuals, which rules serve us and which ones don't.

CHAPTER 4

So who are you really?

If all the world hated you, and believed you wicked, while your own conscience approved you, and absolved you from guilt, you would not be without friends.

Jane Eyre by Charlotte Brontë

I t can be very tricky to work out who you really are. With every one of us experiencing an intensive initial eighteen years of 'training' into the human race, coupled with the many years of rules that follow, we can sometimes lose that all-essential connection to our own core, lose sight of all the components that make us individual and unique.

Self-censoring

What is meant by self-censoring? It's the inner critic – the voice in our heads that questions the thing we almost do or say, deems it inappropriate, wrong, or just too risky, and stops us following it through. Sometimes this is a good judgement call, but often it is something that simply gets us stuck and means we become inauthentic and therefore uncomfortable. People can see that a mile off and then, before we know it, we are in a rut.

Most of us spend a lot of our time unconsciously self-censoring our thoughts and actions. So it's essential that we use a chapter of this book to explore and reconnect with the authentic you – your aspirations, values, metaphorical warts and all, so that we can rebuild our base.

It is not about washing away this training entirely, but simply 'checking in' to see if there's anything that's sneakily slipped off our radar in the years that 'life stuff' has taken over. It is extremely important, if you're going to develop a sound, flexible spectrum of assertive behaviour, to ask that all-important question: are you currently respecting yourself as much as you could be?

↗ brilliant exercise

I'd like you to spend 15 whole minutes thinking solely about yourself between the ages of four and seven. What did you like to do with your time, from the smallest things (like singing in front of the mirror to Madonna songs to the big stuff like BMX contests with friends?) Visualise everything. Go into as much detail as you can.

You may be reminded of some things you haven't recalled for many years. Enjoy it if that happens. Remember you have 15 minutes to immerse yourself. If by chance other details from your childhood come into play that may bring up less pleasant feelings, try not to fight them. Simply allow them to pass and then guide your thoughts back to the pleasurable things that were going on at the time.

After this visualisation, without discussing what has come up with anyone else, make a list of all of the things you remembered or pictured. Or sketch them out below.

_____

_____

_____

_____

The things you loved

The things you loved that you still do will be strongly apparent during this exercise. You may notice some things you no longer do, which you realise that you miss, and then there will be the ones you're glad you don't do anymore.

Note down your observations about this. You may get an emotional sensation, you may smile or giggle, or you may get a warm feeling in your belly. If you get any of these then they are strong indications that this is still something that gives you pleasure so pay attention to these feelings.

Conversely, if you get any other feelings such as dread, a sinking feeling, or feelings of pressure then these are indicative that this is no longer something that motivates you.

_____

_____

_____

_____

_____

Observations

Now see if you can deduce why you liked doing some of these things. For example, I liked to go and lie on my bed and look at or read books because I could escape from the noisiness of the daily household and into another world. To this day the thought of lying undisturbed on a big comfy bed makes me feel very relaxed and safe, whereas the thought of my household being noisy makes me feel quite stressed out.

What does it mean then?

So what can I deduce from this? Well, if I think about this a little more I realise that there are many things in life that still stress me out but that I don't often allow myself the indulgence of lying on my bed and reading. So the question I then ask is 'Why?' The thought, 'Well, I'm often really busy' comes up. Too busy for what? To enjoy the simple pleasures of life? To read and relax?

▶

Once I spend just a little time to unpick what I'm really saying to myself this gets very interesting. What happens if I then think about stretching out on my bed and reading a couple of times a week. What if I simply create a few windows for myself in which to do things like that? That makes me smile because it makes me feel happy.

So this is definitely a core part of me and what I like to do. So then, if I like to do this, why would I deny myself the pleasure of doing it? Is anything more important than doing the things you enjoy in life?

Once you start this process you'll discover a rather wonderfully long list you can choose from to give your life a quick boost or even a few longer moments of indulgence.

Since this is an opportunity to write down your own thoughts and experiences, try not to self-censor but allow yourself to go to the hilarious, the ridiculous, the embarrassing. For example, if you used to tie a scarf around your head and hang bangles from your ears while making your family queue up outside your bedroom to have their fortunes read using a deck of playing cards and peering into a paperweight then put that in there too. No? What, never?! That will just be me then …

Take a good amount of time to think about all of this and really draw your own conclusions from those things you used to enjoy doing as a child. By now you're probably starting to tune back in to who you were as a child. You're likely to be smiling as things come back to you and there are probably a few memories coming up that you haven't thought about for a while.

> Always be a first-rate version of yourself, instead of a second-rate version of somebody else.

Judy Garland, actress

Words and phrases

Write down as many descriptive words or phrases as you can
that relate directly to the younger version of you (these might be
words like 'adventurous', 'into everything', 'loyal', 'a proper little
day-dreamer', etc.). These can be words or phrases that were
used by others too. Don't worry if they appear to contradict each
other as they are all completely valid. None of us is ever just one
thing.

_____

_____

_____

_____

Now see if anything has come up that feels as though it is no
longer something you or anyone else would use to describe
you as you are now. Is there anything that feels like it does not
belong in any way, shape or form? If so, circle it or put a mark
beside it.

How do you feel about the words or phrases you have identified?
Are you pleased that they are no longer representative of you?
Or is there something in there you might like to reclaim? If the
latter rings true then do it. Right now, just think, 'I want to be
that again.' Connect back in to why you enjoy being that thing
and make a conscious decision to reincorporate it into your life
in one way or another from this point forward.

Who or what we wanted to be

All of us have had our role models over the years. It is likely
that we have them now. When you were a child through primary
school, who were your role models, heroes/heroines, or other
people you really looked up to?

_____

_____

_____

_____

What was it about them that made you want to be like them?

_____

_____

_____

_____

brilliant example

I always loved Alannah Currie from the pop group The Thompson Twins because she was a strong and outspoken woman, she dressed as an individual, was a bit of a rebel and was musical and creative. In fact, I'm pretty sure she still is all of those things. These values were also things that were celebrated in my family home. My parents always encouraged creativity, outspokenness and individuality. When I look at myself now these are still the core things that I hold dear in my own life. They are values and aspirations and it's important to me to walk the walk with them. They are also the things I actively encourage other people to value and respect.

Take a look at the list of individuals you have created and annotate it with the qualities of these people that made you hold them up as someone to aspire to be like. Do they start to make you think about your own values in life? The things you speak up to support? The things that make you a happy and fully-functioning person?

Values

It is interesting how our values come about in life. Usually they are things that we have learned along the way and set up for ourselves through experience and having a strong emotional response to those things, either positive or negative.

Values are the things that solidify or break all types of relationship. They are also key things that we have learned directly from our environment, either overtly or covertly. Your values may contain things such as honesty, empathy or respect for other people's points of view. Make a list of them here:

_____

_____

_____

_____

When we don't stick to our own values, that's when we can feel unsettled and annoyed with ourselves. It is very easy to feel restless and upset when somebody else tramples on one of our core values, whether intentionally or not, but when we do it ourselves we can render ourselves quite unforgiveable. From a position of assertiveness this can really knock you off-centre. You can therefore put yourself at a massive disadvantage in dealing with the day-to-day because at your very core something is feeling amiss. If it were a game of chess you'd be vulnerable from all angles. And because this can make us vulnerable, it creates defensiveness, guardedness and a sense of distrust.

So it makes sense then that this is one of the key places from which to monitor your own assertiveness. Values (or indeed morals or ethics as some people may refer to them) act as key indicators of whether or not we are being true to ourselves or holding ourselves, and therefore our own opinions and outlook on life, in high-enough esteem.

Physically and emotionally, our systems are highly adept at signalling to us when we are not respecting these values. Things like tension in the upper body, in particular head, chest, neck and shoulders, can be a real indication that we are stiffening up in order to protect ourselves from some of those 'value tramplers' that are around in our environments. It's almost like we are internally armouring up or shielding.

brilliant definition

The Graves Value Model

Dr Clare Graves was a professor of psychology who spent a lot of his time researching the psychological health of the individual. Graves concluded that there are eight different categories (referred to as systems) of where our personal values are placed, and that we drift around occupying each one at different times in our lives. They are detailed below. As you go through each one, pay attention to how you might relate to these different categories.

Value System One

Defined as beige and representational of instinct.

The concerns here are for survival, with a major emphasis on meeting basic physical needs. One could suggest that this is where the human being is prioritising its own essential needs above anything else.

Value System Two

Defined as purple and representational of tribe.

Here it is the membership of a 'tribe', family or team that takes priority, and people will repress their own needs for the benefit of the tribe. This can mean anything from conscious compromise to a subconscious, and therefore resentful, quashing of personal thoughts and feelings.

Value System Three

Defined by the colour red and representative of power.

When operating from this value system we only really recognise and accept power as a place of negotiation, and therefore interaction with others on a more personal level is limited. This power is the main currency of the relationship. Here there can be a real denial of what is actually happening on a human level and internal indications of true thoughts and feelings can be ignored. This can often be the ground for conflict and the possibility of over-assertiveness coming into play.

Value System Four

Defined as blue and representative of order.

It could be said that to regain the necessary balance, order must be re-established. Hierarchy and knowing the difference between right and wrong is of major importance here. This represents a level of awareness but the question must remain, are the rules that are coming into play here really serving the situation or not? It is important to remain aware when operating within this value system.

Value System Five

Defined as being orange and representative of technology and innovation.

When the status quo becomes turgid and threatens to stop progress, innovative measures are sought through which to drive progress. This is usually the area that sets out to achieve business profit and recognition and humanity can sometimes get overlooked here. However, where there is an opportunity to serve both, this can be a fairly healthy place to operate from.

Value System Six

Defined as green and representative of humanity and the nurturing of it.

It takes into account what is going on for the self and for others so this could be said to tie directly into the flexible middle ground of assertive choice.

Value System Seven

Defined as yellow, standing for all systems.

This is where we can recognise the previous systems and work with them all together. Recognising and using all of the systems will lead to more efficiency and utilising of fewer resources. It helps to create win-wins and is an ideal existence.

Value System Eight

Defined as turquoise and representative of the global view.

There is now a recognition and utilisation of all of the systems within the different cultures and needs of the world, which are today so interconnected. This is trickier to manage and is our most current challenge in day-to-day business. Assertiveness is more important than ever if we are to find ways of making this global community work.

How praise and criticism take effect

When we played as children, both praise and criticism were vital in shaping who we have become. When we're told things like we're being too loud, we're showing off, we are being stupid, we're very good, we're not good enough, we're very clever, we're not clever enough, that we're getting above our stations, that we've been well behaved … and so on, it can have a massive impact.

The same thing can happen as a fully functioning adult. There are still situations where we will look to others for praise, acknowledgement and acceptance, be that at work, in sport, at home, with friends, with partners, with parents (yes, still!). So why do we do it?

Partly, it is learned behaviour and has been so trained into us by the time we reach adulthood that we don't even realise it is happening. So the next time you feel like asking someone 'Is that ok with you?', stop for a minute. Ask yourself why you feel the need to get their approval. Going back to the brilliant Mr Berne, are you acting like an adult and being collaborative? You are. Fantastic.

If not, has that adaptive child taken up residence and made you seek some sort of validation or permission in the way you would with a parent or teacher? If you suspect this is the case then question whether you really need this approval; after all, gone are the days when we promise to obey in wedding vows or work contracts.

When you start to question this seeking of approval you'll discover that nine times out of ten you don't need to seek it.

It's good to start really listening to the self-talk happening in your head, it's there all the time. Notice what you are telling yourself and then question whether it's an adult voice you are hearing or whether that nasty critical parent or worried adaptive child has taken over. This sort of questioning will help you notice and make adjustments so that you can make a conscious choice about how to respond to things, rather than being held hostage by an old, outdated pattern of behaviour.

How we probably view ourselves as assertive

So going back to the beginning of this book then, what does assertiveness actually mean in our own mind's eye? What are the connotations if we go to what we perceive as an assertive place, and is it a positive, negative or neutral thing?

The chances are that the way you feel when you assert yourself in a challenging situation is not as strong as you think. That is because we are experiencing ourselves from the internal and the rest of the world experiences our external persona.

brilliant exercise

1   Visualise for yourself what you think you look like, sound like and how you come across when you are being assertive. Jot down some notes here:

   _____

   _____

   _____

   _____

   _____

2   Is there anything that feels scary or uncomfortable about behaving in this way? What are the connotations for you, either positive or negative?

   _____

   _____

   _____

   _____

   _____

3 And how true are these visualisations? If you're not sure you could ask someone you trust, but only as a one-off for this exercise! Let's remember not to go back to making a habit of checking in with others about how you are coming across.

Are there any surprises when you really sit down and think about or discuss what your own personal assertive behaviour looks like? Is there a possibility of anything coming across differently from how you intended it to? And if so, in what ways?

Record your thoughts below.

_____

_____

_____

_____

Thinking assertively

Now if you are of a cynical persuasion you aren't going to believe the next sentence, but I assure you it is true.

By just thinking yourself more assertive you can become so.

I know that sounds too easy but it's been proven many times over. Ask any athlete about their core preparation for a big event and one of the most important things they will identify as a success factor is imagining themselves winning – whether it's the 100 metres, the FA Cup or Wimbledon.

Every athlete will spend time just before the event imagining success. Combining this with their particular sporting prowess enables their bodies to know what they need to do to reach the goal.

It's the same for you. You simply need to trust it. So next time you are preparing for a situation where you need to use your assertiveness skills then, just before you go in, think 'assertive' to yourself and it will really help you to get off the starting blocks in the right way. And the start is always the hardest part. Once you start the only important thing to remember is to keep on going.

brilliant recap

- Think about who you were as a child – what were your likes and dislikes and do they match up with the adult version of you?

- Allow yourself the time to regularly do the things you genuinely take pleasure in doing – take the lead from what you enjoyed doing as a child

- Know your own values and take care of them by ensuring you have set boundaries so they don't cause a negative effect on you

- Have the confidence that you can start to gauge for yourself whether your own behaviour is appropriate or not in a given situation – always trust your instinct!

- The assertiveness level you feel internally is not always fully representative of how your assertiveness is being perceived externally

CHAPTER 5

Over-assertiveness and over-compensation

I'm a real 'go, go' person ... I'd make myself crazy by pushing too hard. It's important to pull back the reins a little bit and get in touch with what's inside.

Shelley Long, actress

When we aren't as assertive as we would like to be, and we push down those uneasy feelings that result from that, it is only a matter of time before we 'blow.' This usually leads to over-assertive behaviour, which can be just as debilitating as being under-assertive.

So now we scoot right across to the farthest point on the spectrum (or rather off it) and explore the place where we push back too much, the place where we are overly assertive, the place where we might blow our tops and lose control. This is the place where we speak too forcefully, it is the place where we might lose our tempers, lose the plot, see red, flip our lids and other such phrases.

It is the place where we are driven mainly by our egos, and our usual rationale can fly off the radar before we have time to catch it. Then we have to do a lot of caretaking to make things alright again once things have calmed back down, which can be utterly exhausting.

It sounds like such an easy thing to do – to rise above things – but in real life it is of course far less easy … as illustrated by some of the examples over the page.

brilliant example

Over-assertiveness when presenting

Picture this: a room full of about 200 people sipping coffees and orange juices, some nibbling on Danish pastries, eagerly awaiting an inspiring presentation about how to Manage Your Team in a Recession.

The man, Mike, steps in front of the audience. He is confident and looking very dapper indeed in his tailored suit. Everyone feels confident that he can hold the room and he does at the beginning. It has started well …

Then Mike suddenly seems to flip into arrogance. This arrogance appears to have been kicked off by a left-of-field question from a woman in the front row of the audience. 'So what is the quickest solution?', she asks simply. He replies with a scoff followed quickly by, 'Didn't you just hear what we were talking about? The main thing we need to do in this recession is spend time on teams. If your attention is on the quickest thing then you're hurtling towards disaster. That's all I have to say about that! So back to the point I was making …'

The room suddenly becomes tense. In some respects it's a relief to hear a presenter get straight to the point with a question, and with such honesty too. But something is amiss. It feels too harsh, too rude, just a little bit too much honesty. It's probably teetering into the over-assertive edge of the spectrum, where behaviour feels more fixed and certainly less generous.

In fact, the behaviour that has just been displayed is entirely about what is going on for Mike, rather than being coupled with what might be going on for the questioner. And that's what makes it feel amiss.

Why?

Think back to The Graves Value Model in the previous chapter (see p. 72) and it backs up our assertiveness theory – that if we don't strive for the flexible middle ground, the see-saw balance between human beings, we can end up very stuck at one end not knowing quite how to re-establish the balance.

After the presentation I ask Mike how it all went for him. 'Well it was fine up until the woman in the front row asked that stupid question. Then it all went downhill.' This is a classic response. It feels like the whole downfall of his presentation was due to her. And in some respects it was. If it hadn't been for her question then the well-established flow would have carried on right until the end.

But of course life isn't like that, and in particular presentations are not like that. The unexpected can always happen and regularly does. The downfall is down to the presenter.

If Mike had chosen just a slightly different response then the presentation would not have gone downhill at all. That's the thing with over-assertiveness. It feels like we were forced into our response and it is all the fault or consequence of somebody else. It feels like we have no choice and it feels like our emotional response takes over, dragging us with it like an over-excited puppy on a lead.

We end up 'pinging', and it does feel like a sudden ping, into over-assertiveness because it feels like we have no choice in that particular moment – either in terms of the responses we can have or the situations we are in. Sometimes it can be both.

In the case of this particular presentation, Mike did confess that he didn't like questions while he was on his train of thought. He was afraid that he might lose the thread and that caused him to be a little on-edge. He had perfected the art of an exterior calmness but deep down he was dreading the moment that question flew at him from out of the blue.

Doing it differently

So is there anything Mike could have done differently in order to feel better about his handling of the question and therefore take care of the audience and how they were feeling within all of this?

Well, firstly, if you do have those areas where you struggle then begin to explore some of the possibilities around the responses available.

The second thing to do is try to allow for the unexpected to happen. This allows flexibility. If you aim for perfection when presenting then perfection is less likely to happen than if you aim for imperfection.

And in Mike's case he could have simply started the presentation by making it clear that he would take any questions at the end, which would have avoided the whole situation.

 'If you hold on to the handle', she said, 'it's easier to maintain the illusion of control. But it's more fun if you just let the wind carry you.'

Brian Andreas, writer and painter

That quote is great advice for life and it's great advice for a presentation, because through letting go of being 'in control' you allow anything to happen and therefore the flexible middle ground that ensues enables an appropriately assertive presence.

brilliant tip

If you know you are entering a situation where your defences may be tested, try thinking through some solutions in advance. Using the example above, here's how Mike could have prepared himself better:

Issue	An under-assertive response might be:	An over-assertive response might be:	Some options in the middle ground:
A question in the middle of the presentation.	Freezing on the spot. Not being able to think of an answer.	To get defensive or to humiliate the questioner.	1. To say 'Good question, thank you. Anyone else got any thoughts on that?' 2. At the beginning of the presentation establish when you would like questions to be asked. 3. Answer the question politely and move on (however ridiculous it may sound to you).

Issue	An under-assertive response might be:	An over-assertive response might be:	Some options in the middle ground:
Someone who keeps talking through the presentation.	To ignore them and let them get under your skin.	To confront them and ask them to be quiet.	1. Walk over to near where they are in the room but carry on with the presentation, avoiding eye contact with the culprit. 2. Simply stop talking for a moment.
Someone who keeps asking questions and it feels like they are trying to catch you out.	To lose your train of thought, keep eye contact and let them dominate the presentation.	Starting to accuse them of trying to catch you out in an open manner.	1. Acknowledge their question and then take it to the larger group to include everyone in your response. 2. Ask the questioner to elaborate further on their question to give you time to hold your nerve and think about the appropriate response.

▶ brilliant example

Over-assertiveness on a date

James had been single for about six months. His last relationship hadn't ended too well and he had been enjoying some time on his own before he decided to 'get back in the game', as it were. After about a month on a couple of internet dating sites he came across Sarah, whom he thought was gorgeous. So, after a bit of flirtatious emailing and texting, they decided to meet up and see how it all went.

Before they met, though, there were a few things that were concerning James. Firstly, Sarah was sending lots of texts with xxx's at the end. 'That's all very nice', he was thinking, 'but we haven't actually met each other yet.' After about five of these texts he thought it best to manage Sarah's expectations a little better.

So James sent her a text saying, 'I'm really looking forward to meeting you tomorrow. Let's just have a cup of coffee and chat. I would like to take this one step at a time and see how it goes.' Relieved, he sent the text, only to have a beep back less than a minute later: 'Absolutely. I can't wait to meet you xxx.'

James decided to leave any more communication until they were face to face. Initially, James was sitting on a café terrace on London's South Bank. Sarah was running late and had texted to say, 'Sorry but the trains are all delayed at my end x.' 'Just one kiss?' thought James, 'maybe she took some time to think and now understands what I meant. Phew.' Famous last words …

When Sarah arrived she planted a huge kiss on James' cheek. James felt a little awkward but carried on saying hello, getting her a coffee and chatting with her in a friendly manner. After about 10 minutes of conversation Sarah put her hand on James' leg stating, 'I just knew we'd get on so well. I don't like to mess around when I know something is right,' and promptly kissed him passionately. 'So what shall we do this evening honey?', she asked.

▶

What happened?

There could be various phrases applied to Sarah, from simply a bit over-keen to a complete and utter bunny boiler! Actually, it appears that what happened on this date was a typical case of over-assertiveness. Sarah, it would appear upon later conversations with James, was incredibly nervous on dates. She had quite low self-esteem and hadn't quite been able to believe it when James contacted her via the website.

Sarah had thought that if she 'took charge of the matter' she could make things work out and convince James that she was confident and in charge. She couldn't have been further from the truth. He ran a mile, unsurprisingly. However, he did get in touch with her to talk about why he'd run a mile and, although Sarah was pretty embarrassed about the whole thing, at least their conversation gave both of them some food for thought. That was pretty assertive behaviour on James' part. It allowed a move forward while staying in the middle ground.

It's extremely common on dates for people to be nervous. And it is also extremely common for one person to feel like they need to take charge and 'look after' the whole experience. By doing this, however, the shared experience becomes lost. It is far better to communicate between the two people concerned, using questions and really listening to what one another has to say. Only by getting some clarity about what is going on for the other person in the equation can the appropriate level of behaviour be chosen. Conversation is key. It seems like an obvious thing to say, but when we get caught up in our own emotional anxieties we can forget that basic part of human relationships.

Issue	An under-assertive response might be:	An over-assertive response might be:	Some options in the middle ground:
Being nervous before a date.	Calling the date off or postponing indefinitely.	Texting or calling in an overfamiliar way or dominating the situation.	1. Engaging in conversation beforehand and stating that you would like to keep the meeting short. 2. Saying out loud at the beginning of the date that you are a little nervous. 3. Replacing the word 'date' in your mind with 'meeting up' or 'a quick coffee and chat', or suchlike.
Wanting to bring the date to a close.	To say nothing but wait until the other person says something, feeling more and more uncomfortable as time goes on.	To finish it abruptly and say something like, 'Right, I need to go. See you soon.' Or, 'I'm not really that into you so I'm going to leave. Sorry.'	1. To manage the expectations of the other person by saying something prior to or at the beginning of the date, such as, 'I will have to leave at 5pm today', or 'I would feel more comfortable keeping this date to just a few hours.' 2. Being clear about leaving while remaining respectful. 'It's been a lovely opportunity to meet you. Thanks. I will be in touch.' And then get in touch not too long afterwards, even if just to say a respectful 'thanks but no thanks.'

▶ **brilliant** example

Over-assertiveness in the workplace

There is a lot of this in the workplace and most of it appears to be a result of a lack of communication.

The example here is about a woman called Claire who was a PA to the head of a marketing company and spent most of her time stomping around the office, huffing, puffing, swearing and slamming doors. Most people were terrified of her. It was only when I found myself in a queue for the loos at a Christmas 'do' that I realised what was really going on with Claire. Up to that point I'd found any excuse not to be around her, but I was somewhat trapped in the fateful queue that Christmas.

As I sidled up to Claire mumbling, 'Alright?', and hoping not to get much of a response, I noticed she had been crying. 'It seems not', I said to her and she turned to face me. 'Nobody likes me at work. Hardly anyone has spoken to me all night', she sniffled. No wonder, I thought, you terrify people!

What was really going on?

Actually it materialised that Claire was being given a bit of a hard time by her boss. Most of the stomping around that made us think she was a stroppy woman with an anger management problem turned out to be a terrified woman, who didn't know where or whom to turn to.

What made things harder for Claire was that she was a single parent and had no family living near her. She was feeling very alone and 'like she was invisible.' If we think back to Berne's model of transactional analysis as mentioned in Chapter 3 of this book (see p. 40), what was happening at work was that Claire's boss was taking the role of the Critical Parent, which was having the effect of creating the Rebellious Child in Claire.

She admitted that her boss made her feel like an incompetent child and, since she was feeling pretty incompetent in her personal life too, she was left feeling terrified and completely at sea. The stomping around was the only 'voice' she could find to try and cry for help. And of course that wasn't serving her.

Claire was failing to realise that by her expressive outbursts following these incidents in her boss' office, people did not want to approach her as she appeared angry and unreasonable. In actual fact she appeared to be somewhat unhinged at times. Nobody realised that what she actually needed was some help and support.

Thinking about this in terms of the assertiveness spectrum and the response choices available to Claire, it is interesting to look at the realistic options she had.

Options

Firstly, in terms of dealing with her boss, the obvious option is the one that links straight back to Eric Berne's theory – respond like a very calm adult, regardless of what is coming at you. This is easier said than done, and so I offer another 'trick', or metaphor, to help with this.

In order to keep some distance between you and your emotions in this situation it may help to visualise someone else's emotional outburst as them unpacking a grocery bag on the table. It is a very full grocery bag but it is theirs. If you think of the tins of beans as representing their emotions and upset, then do we want to carry those other 'tins of emotions' that

▶

don't actually belong in our shopping bag? I would suggest not. Therefore visualise them, see them, acknowledge them, but under no circumstances should you pick them up and carry them around. Your own tins of 'beans' are heavy enough.

Keeping language neutral can also help with this. If someone starts to criticise and complain it can be incredibly useful simply to use their language and reflect back to them what they have said.

Taking an example from Claire's story, one day her boss exploded at her and said: 'I don't understand how you have time to take personal phone calls when the workload is piling up.' Close to tears, Claire put her phone away and started work on the next task on her 'to do' list. What her boss didn't know is it had been her son's school on the phone because he wasn't feeling well.

In this instance, had Claire been taught how to be more assertive she could have responded: 'I am very conscious of our workload and I would like to reassure you that I wouldn't take a personal call unless it was of the utmost importance, which in that case it was. I have now dealt with the situation and I am just about to complete that report you asked for. Is there anything else you need?'

A response like this doesn't really leave the boss with anywhere to go and can mean that both Clare and her boss can get on with the rest of the day. Hopefully it will also have given her boss pause for thought to realise that Clare is a conscientious worker and would only take an urgent call, which in turn would enable him to have more faith in her and treat her as an adult and partner in helping him get through the workload, rather than as a naughty child who needs constant monitoring and criticism.

Anyone, whatever their position in any communication dynamic, can pull things back on track by taking the position of the calm, attentive adult. It enables your attention to stay with the other person and the dynamic becomes two-way. Win-win. Balanced.

For the record, and in order to give you the classic happy ending, Claire and I actually ended up discussing all of these options and theories for a good two hours squashed on a step opposite the ladies. She worked hard to change her tactics and people's responses towards her changed significantly. I still see her actually. She is a really nice woman and a good friend. The levelling that the circumstances allowed that night in the toilet queue provided a real turning point for Claire. But, as she puts it herself, she had to hit rock bottom (tears and loneliness at a Christmas party) before she could really start to see what else was possible. Here's hoping that isn't the case for everyone.

brilliant example

Over-assertiveness in a restaurant (or similar)

Families and food ... birthday celebrations and restaurants. These words can send shivers up the hardiest of spines, and for good reason. Over-assertive behaviour in a public place with a decent-sized audience can be one of the trickiest things to have to deal with in the heat of the moment. And it can also be one of the most cringe-worthy.

Imagine a wonderful restaurant in a highly swanky area. The table has been booked for several weeks because if you don't get in early there is no way you will get a table for 12 at short notice. The family have RSVP'd, final numbers counted, presents bought, posh frocks and glitter embodied, suits suited and ties tied. Everyone is decked out in the finest attire and they're all in the car giggling and looking forward to a good family catch up 'avec vin.' The night is bound to go swimmingly ... isn't it?!

So why, oh why, oh why do most of us, despite playing out the charade described above, have a sinking feeling in the pit of our stomachs in the cab ride there, just waiting for 'that moment' to happen on the ever-fateful family celebratory meal out? If it isn't the wrong starter (too hot, too cold), main (too rare, overdone), pudding (too big, too small), wine (dry, sweet), waitress (friendly, grumpy), cushion (hard, soft), music (loud, rubbish), or whatever else there is to be debated over, it is some through-gritted-teeth ▶

remark that bounces across the table at some point or other, just waiting to be seized upon by the person for whom it is most definitely 'not intended' (honest!), who has usually, by this point, consumed that one glass of wine more than they should have and reacts in the extreme. Happy memories? Well, maybe not.

Over-assertive behaviour is rife when no family member will give up their well-preened position or pride within the family pecking order without a cross word or ten. Or a passive aggressive sulk. Or a storm out. Or all three. Sound familiar?

With so many witnesses to such a delicate situation, how is such a thing manageable within this fluid assertiveness spectrum of which we have so far spoken? Surely it can't be that simple? Well ... no. But it is possible. Forearmed can only be good, right? Right!

So what can you do?

Well, what can you do? You know best here! You certainly can't always prevent or fix the thing, but you can certainly attempt to manage it. So let's start to put everything we have spoken about into a pot of 'tips for the table':

Some tips for the table

1   It is what it is. Try not to put the 'it has to be perfect' expectation on the evening. It will inevitably go the same way as that uncontrollable presentation if you do that. If things aren't up to scratch, so be it.

2   If you must complain about something (a dish, seating, or whatever) do it discreetly, turned away from the table to save the embarrassment of the restaurant staff or any member of the family. Keep it short and to the point and don't get personal about it.

3   If a family grizzle does start to emerge between people, try not to get entangled, even if you mean to 'calm things down.' Let the people involved have their space. The less attention the incident is given, the less it will thrive. A little like not fanning a flame.

4   If any insult flies across the table, remember the concept of the

tins of beans. People will always dump their stuff on the table, metaphorically speaking, and none of us can do anything about that. But we don't have to pick it up or engage with them – that is an option that we have some control over.

5 Stay adult. Despite family history, do avoid, if you can, any of the parent/child dynamics, even if you are dealing with a parent/child relationship.

6 Breathe! And smile, but not too much (just in case someone takes it the wrong way …).

A quick note on assumptions

The assumptions we can jump to about people and any given situation can really get us into trouble. We will often base our interpretations on our own historical references, forgetting that everyone else has their own individual set. We can become so convinced that we are right that we forget to check in with the actual facts, and instead treat our assumptions as the facts and then react accordingly.

When it comes to over-assertive behaviour, often our own interpretation and our own inner critic will have us believe something that can be quite different from what is going on in actuality.

brilliant example

Marcus is someone who frowns. He frowns a lot. He frowns because he has a very handsome face but this handsome face needs glasses, badly. Marcus refuses to wear these glasses because he still wants to feel he looks good, which means he ends up frowning. It is that simple.

One day Alex came in to the office. Alex was fairly new and lacked some self-confidence. Alex became convinced that Marcus disliked him, thought ▶

he was rubbish at his job and didn't ever want to talk to him because every time Marcus looked at Alex he was frowning. Marcus thought Alex was snobby because he never spoke to him.

One day, when Marcus asked Alex if he could have a look at a piece of work with him and give him his opinion, Alex snapped, 'Oh you want to talk to me now eh? Now that you need my help?' Marcus was stunned. This was confirmation for him that Alex was indeed snobby and 'up himself.' Alex thought Marcus was unbelievably cheeky for using him in this way even though it was blatantly obvious that Marcus really didn't like Alex.

The moral of this story is that Marcus really should just get some glasses. Or at the very least make it known to people why he frowns so much. And Alex? I'm giving him a copy of this book.

When your own brain leaps to an assumption, always check it out. We humans do have a tendency to think everything around us is all about us, when in actual fact usually it isn't.

---

brilliant recap

- Keep an open and honest channel of communication as much as you can and listen to how other people feel or think about any situation
- Don't aim for perfection as it is unachievable
- If there feels like a lack of choice in terms of responses available, think about models such as Berne's transactional analysis
- Don't pick up or engage with other people's emotional issues (or their tins of beans) if they push them at you
- Listen to and acknowledge the opinions of others, even if you don't agree with them

PART 2

Taking charge
of it all

CHAPTER 6

Talking the talk

Be who you are and say what
you feel, because those who
mind don't matter and those who
matter don't mind.

Dr Seuss, children's author and
cartoonist

Firstly, when we are small we work as one unit – everything is connected; all of the systems in our bodies are naturally supporting each other and working together. We are also fearless – we haven't yet learned to be anxious or afraid. As we grow we learn these fears, which create tension in the body and therefore a 'disconnect' with our voices (an easy example of this is the tension we can hold in our shoulders and necks, which immediately limits the space in our throats where voice is created). So when we do need to use our voices to assert ourselves, quite often we will over-compensate by pushing, will fly to over-assertive behaviour and hurt our vocal system. Babies simply 'say' what they need there and then in the moment and it is dealt with. There is no need to hold tension because of not 'saying' something or having let it all out at once. This non-productive vocal behaviour only happens in adults.

Pandora's voice-box

Whenever I do vocal work with people, whether in a corporate or acting environment, the same issues tend to come up again and again. I have developed my own analogy for this and I call it the Pandora's (Voice) Box effect. I'll explain why.

In the Greek myth, Pandora is the first woman and, like Eve, she is tempted to do a forbidden act. Zeus gives her and her new husband a box with a huge lock on it and tells them both never to open it. He also gives them the key. Of course, Pandora's curiosity gets the better of her and she takes the key and opens the box, unleashing all sorts of horrors into the world such as disease, envy, anger, hate, etc. They fly out before she can catch them. When she tells her husband what she has done she goes to show him the now-empty box but there, remaining, is hope. Pandora then unleashes hope from the box and out into the world too.

I love this story. When things get on top of me I always remember it – there is always hope. It's a nice image. But why does it equate in my mind so strongly with voice and our associations to it?

Well, think of the lid of the voice box being in the throat. We are often terrified to 'open the box' and fully speak out for fear of what will happen (unleashing our own horrors into the world – whatever they may be). However, if we were to fully unleash everything, what we would get at the end would be lovely and positive (hope).

But something profoundly strong in us doesn't trust this, so most of us walk around stifling our own voices in one way or another – saying nothing, choking things back and sometimes not even breathing properly. It's as if we are terrified that if we let go the whole world will descend into chaos. If we let go we will reveal our true selves and that has to be a bad thing, right? If we let go, we might just make too much noise or make a difference

our entire system healthy. A lack of oxygen to the body can exacerbate stress, depression, lethargy and other such states. Secondly, it is important that we have breath to create sound within our vocal chords and are thus able to fully respond authentically to any situation – be that with a whisper or a yell. And thirdly, we need to breathe properly in order that our whole system is responsive and alert.

So, even though by the very nature of being alive we know we are breathing, it is definitely worth seeing if we are breathing fully and properly.

The key steps to breathing

Breathe down into your diaphragm, expanding the lungs as you go. Beware of shallow, chesty breathing. Inhale through the nose gently and exhale through the mouth gently. Slow your breathing down. Keep your chin dipped into your chest but not forced – that is the middle place between thrusting your head and neck forward or backwards. Relax, smile and allow your breath to take as much space as it needs to.

brilliant tip

If you catch yourself not breathing properly, or panicking before a meeting, pitch, presentation or other important conversation, then be careful when 'taking deep breaths.' It is the thing most people say to each other in these situations and it is definitely something we tend to say to ourselves, but there is an important distinction to be made. Don't make the inhale the point of focus – if you do this you are likely to add to your anxiety, and in worst-case scenarios it can cause hyperventilation. Instead, focus on exhaling as fully as you can and then replenishing the breath with a gentle inhale, not a sucking one. Exhale as fully and as easily as you can and try not to push. This way you are breathing out and releasing nervous energy in the form of carbon dioxide, not taking more in.

Language limitations

There are times in life when we just cannot find the words to say what we want to say. It might be that we feel we just don't have the language in the heat of the moment, it might be that we feel we're not communicating what we can see in our mind's eye or we may simply become tongue-tied altogether. In these situations it is a good idea to say what is going on. Here are some of the possible things to say in the moment:

1 'I can't find the right words to say just now. I'm going to take a moment/ten minutes (or another time of your choosing).'

2 'I don't think this is coming over clearly/how I'd like it to. Let me try to say it a different way.'

3 'I'm feeling a little bit tongue-tied. I need to take some time to think about this.'

4 'My mind is blank. I'm going to take myself off to think about what I want to say clearly. I will be back in ten minutes.'

Usually these language limitations only happen because we have got what is the equivalent of stage fright in a moment where something happens that pushes our buttons, for one reason or another.

When we get 'stage fright', and this is not just something that happens to dancers, singers and actors but something that can happen to anybody when they are in a pressured work situation and they need to make some sort of positive impact on others, our breathing is interrupted.

Once our breathing is interrupted so are our thought patterns, our digestive systems knot up and our nervous system goes into overdrive. We can feel hot, sweaty, nauseous, our chest can feel tight, we might go red and flushed, we panic and the upper part

and sound. It's a useful trick before an important presentation or meeting. A lovely side effect of this, I have noticed, is that it also focuses the mind and therefore clarifies thought, meaning we can make a far more assertive decision and impact when we choose to in these kind of situations.

Yawning

In British culture, at least, a big open yawn and stretch in public might be considered rude and offensive, but in private I would urge you to yawn away. Just the sheer mention of the word may already have you yawning as you read, so there is no time like the present (unless at this moment you are on a really crowded train or something).

Doing the biggest, loudest, most over-the-top yawns we can muster is a fantastic way to get us breathing in a more supportive way. Yawning releases stagnant air and any anxieties we may be harbouring along with it. Yawning also gets us to open our mouths and release any vocal tension, in particular the tension that has a tendency to reside in the neck and throat.

By opening up these muscles and releasing air, we are exercising the muscles that permit us to open our mouths properly when we speak, so enabling a clear and more rounded sound. By assisting with effective breath support it helps us to produce a much richer sound and have a stronger impact on those listening.

Whispering

If we whisper when we tell a story we can create intrigue and suspense. Technically when we whisper we also have to form the words in a much clearer manner in order to be understood. Whenever you need to make an important point in front of a large group, be it a business pitch, proposal at a meeting or a speech at a wedding, it is a great idea to exaggeratedly whisper your way through it first. I would recommend doing this privately of course.

Not only does whispering really get our mouths chewing around the vocal sounds so as to maximise the effect they have on people, but it also links us directly to our diaphragm breathing, which is a more supportive and 'connected' place from which to deliver any sort of information. Practise doing this and notice what differences whispering can make to your vocal delivery.

brilliant tip

Many people have a tendency to get to the end of their point having begun to exercise assertive behaviour only to fall away at the end. It is almost like their brain is saying they're done before they actually are and their mouth follows suit, so destroying any positive effects made when delivering the bulk of the content.

Always make sure that you end what you say, in any situation, with power and hit your punctuation (even if you aren't talking from the written page). Envisage telling a story to a young child. You would most certainly give them their 'happily ever after' with as much dedication as you would their 'once upon a time' because you wouldn't want to lose the impact of the whole tale right at the end. So why do it in your everyday affairs?

Pay special attention to how you conclude your points of view, make statements and engage in conversation in your daily life and notice how much more seriously people take you and your opinions.

CHAPTER 7

Walking the walk

No one saves us but ourselves.
No one can and no one may. We
ourselves must walk the path.

Buddha

What is interesting about the human condition is that we understand things intellectually very quickly and very well. What is even more curious is that it is quite another matter when it comes to us actually doing them.

Harvard professor Howard Gardner identifies well with this when he speaks about his theory of the multiple intelligences of the human being. Gardner suggests that man understands the world through several different intelligences, not just the cognitive. Included in there are the likes of spatial intelligence and bodily-kinesthetic intelligence, which would suggest that our physical understanding of the world may be different from our logical understanding. This would make sense of how emotions can overtake our 'logical' thought processes and it would make sense as to why our instinct is usually right.

In the acting world it is certainly true that actors can understand a range of techniques very easily in concept alone but it is a significant shift to get into any performance space and 'live' the changes. Sport is in the same territory.

What we really need to do is start walking the walk to create shifts in the less helpful patterns currently linked to non-assertive behaviour.

As with every learning exercise, in order to make this chapter work the best it can for you, you will need to practise the exercises and tools. You will need to speak and you will need to move. There's no getting away from it if you want things to shift for the better.

It's all about what we do

What we communicate physically makes a huge impact. For the most part, we don't really have to pay much attention to our body language because we are working holistically without even having to think about it.

Sometimes, though, we need to make conscious some of those things we take for granted in order to maximise our impact or achieve a more productive outcome. This is particularly true if we have some difficult internal thoughts or feelings accompanying the situation. Our body tends to let on that something is amiss very quickly and human beings are extremely astute at detecting these signals from one another.

There have been many so-called 'rules' about body language and its meanings but, of course, two things need to be noted here. One, we really are trying to challenge rules in this book because rules tend to hinder the human working as a whole rather than help things. Two, there can be a lot of variations in the patterns of body language depending upon culture and historical references so it is impossible to have any definitive statements. We can only have guidelines. These 'rules' should be accompanied with a mental question mark where possible and there is always room to adapt depending on your position and your individual situation.

↗ brilliant impact

Working with intentions

So now it is time to steal a key technique from the acting world and use it in a real-life, day-to-day context. It is crucial to note that acting is not, as it is very commonly misunderstood to be, pretending. Acting is being. Acting is being truthful, warts and all. It is about being human. It is about being flexible, responsive and imperfect. Once this is clear in people's minds, anything that relates to acting throughout this book should be taken simply as a state of being in a truthful way within life itself and not one that involves pretending or 'acting' as if you are somebody else.

Intentions are a major part of any actor's toolkit. They are the reason that anything ever happens on stage or screen. There is always an intention behind what is happening, major or minor, as in life. For example, in the well-known Shakespeare play *Romeo and Juliet*, Romeo's intention at the balcony is to woo Juliet. Everything he does has this end-goal in mind. So let's relate this to the day-to-day in our life and, more specifically, the world of assertiveness. If you are going into a meeting simply thinking, 'It's just another meeting, it will be boring – let's get through it as fast as possible and get back to that pile of work on my desk,' then that is exactly what the body will be communicating to the world, or in this case the meeting room.

Walk into a meeting with the intention of driving a specific issue forward or getting a decision on a project and you will conduct yourself quite differently, even without thinking once about what your body language is communicating. It just happens by the very fact that we have that intention.

When you are clear about what yours is/are then you will likely operate with more decisiveness and awareness. You are more likely to be outspoken about certain things because they affect the outcome you walked in aiming to get. There is a kind of pull that dictates very clearly what is necessary

▶

at any given time. Aristotle and his definition of assertiveness[1] would be extremely pleased with that one!

To use some sporting analogies in order to help frame this concept further, it is the difference between running a race just to take part and running a race to win a gold medal or get a personal best. It is the difference between playing a game of football just to take part and playing with the intention of scoring a hat trick in the first half.

The differences in outcome are pretty significant here, just as they are in life. Give a so-called 'monkeys' about any situation and your presence, confidence and assertiveness levels will inevitably rise. Your body simply responds to what your mind is doing. They are inherently linked and it makes sense that we start to become more conscious of this and use it to our advantage.

So, breaking it down then, here are just some of the components to be aware of when going out into the world to operate from an assertive and confident place:

Eye contact

Generally we are all quite hard-wired to give an appropriate level of eye contact (not too staring, but enough). However, it is important to note where we can inadvertently get caught out with this one.

Often if a person is feeling under-confident eye contact will diminish, and so it is important to make it more consciously rather than relying on habit. If one feels confronted then eye contact tends to go to one extreme or the other (either wide-eyed rabbit/staring or a complete withdrawal of it).

1   'Anybody can become angry – that is easy, but to be angry with the right person and to the right degree and at the right time and for the right purpose, and in the right way – that is not within everybody's power and is not easy.'

Another thing to be aware of is the proximity and how that can limit eye contact. If we are too close to someone often our eye contact goes and we can forget the option of simply moving to one side or creating more space to allow for a stronger eye connection to happen. The other thing to be aware of is the fact that if there is a group of people around a table, or other, we tend to forget the people immediately to one side (left and right). Too much eye contact here might be a little strange but this is simply a reminder to include them with a light glance.

On the whole, in group situations spread your eye contact. It has the amazing effect of helping you to feel in balance and in charge and is therefore key in raising confidence. If you want or need to make a strong impact, then ensure your eye contact does not get stuck in any one place. The assertive effect is profound both for you and for others.

An important cultural difference with eye contact

Normally good, measured eye contact is considered assertive and respectful. However, it is important to note where some differences lie so as to avoid miscommunication or misguided negative assumptions. In some Caribbean, Japanese and Australian Aboriginal cultures younger people are instructed (and therefore it has become one of their ingrained social 'rules') not to look at someone in the eye when being spoken to by someone older or hierarchically above them.

Facial expressions

We read a lot on people's faces and we can make a lot of assumptions, both positive and negative, about what is being expressed. Our faces can be a great way to express what is really going on, but can also let us down when it comes to assertiveness unless we have some awareness about what messages they are sending out.

The smile

For the most part, we all love a good smile and we love a good laugh. It can make us feel safe and accepted. It can make us feel approved of and liked. From the moment we're born, we are faced with people goo-ing and gaa-ing into our prams, cots and buggies and very quickly we learn to do it right back. It's one of the main ways we bond as human beings and on the whole it is an incredibly positive bit of body language.

But, if we are not careful, our laughter and smiles can also undermine how effective we can be when it comes to assertiveness. Many of us smile without even being aware that we are doing it. We smile because inside we're worried that we won't be liked or approved of. It's a way of keeping a professional boundary between us and the world, as well as acting as a bond, particularly in work situations. None of us wants to be perceived as miserable, unhelpful or unapproachable, so the smile sneaks its way onto our faces when we're not looking. Well, kind of.

If you need to stand your ground on an issue, present some serious numbers to a room of investors, or voice a major concern in a meeting then the smile can dramatically weaken your impact. Try it. Try talking about a serious issue with a smile on your face and then gradually smile less and less and you will actually feel the difference it makes.

If you are someone who is a natural grinner then it is next to impossible to stop grinning completely, but it is possible to grin to a smaller degree. Bear this in mind when you need to assert yourself and have a decent amount of presence in a room. Bear this in mind when you need to say no. If you want to be taken seriously, let your face back up that message.

The well-known frown

Just like smiling, there are some people who are natural frowners. We can frown for all sorts of reasons: we're tired; we're worried;

we're thinking; we're upset, irritated or annoyed; we need new glasses; the sun is in our eyes; and probably a whole host of other possibilities.

Usually, though, if someone is on the receiving end of a frown the assumption is a negative one. We can feel intimidated or a little scared. This person on the other end of the communication dynamic is not someone to be messed with! That is fine if that is the message you want to send out but usually it isn't useful. If we were to hang the frown and what it conveys on our assertiveness spectrum then it could be considered overly assertive behaviour (if we take the intention or the reason out of the equation, that is).

So it seems that the best way to manage a frown, whether it is on your face or somebody else's, is to admit it is there. If you know you are a frowner, then it is a good idea to manage the other person's expectations around it. I am one of life's big brow-knitters. Not because I am grumpy but because, one, I'm a big thinker and two, it's a family trait. So I do tend to be very aware of how other people are affected by it, particularly if they approach me when I am in the middle of working on something. If they don't know me well, I will make a conscious effort to smile to combat the effect, and I will usually say something like, 'Sorry about the brow, I'm not that formidable I promise', in a light-hearted manner.

If someone else is frowning then it is a good idea to ask a question if you are concerned that it will get in the way of the communication exchange. Something like, 'How is everything with you?' will give you a better gauge rather than going straight in with, 'What's the matter?' If somebody is a natural frowner then a question of this directness may cause some offence.

Of course, if there is a negotiation happening over workload or a push back of a boundary and the frown emerges during this, it can give some indication of the impact the situation is directly having on the other person. It's all about context and relating the behaviour to the specific situation.

Practising it all

It is a big ask to request your system to make a change to an old habitual tendency in the heat of a highly important moment, particularly in front of colleagues or people who matter to your work or life in one way or another. I wouldn't recommend for a moment that you leap straight in and try something dramatically different when the stakes are high.

What I would recommend is that you start by watching situations, watching how people interact with one another and seeing which words, behaviours and facial expressions create different tones and moods within a particular context. Then start to make the shifts in your mind.

Consider possibilities and be aware of other people using them and then try them out where it really doesn't matter if you wobble, for example in situations such as sending food back in a restaurant or changing your drink at a bar. Only once you are familiar with the other options you have, both in mind and within your system on a visceral level, should you start to make those changes in the situations where it really matters that you make that assertive impact for the better.

Keep moving forward ... literally

The term 'moving things forward' appears to have a very clear meaning in our heads. It means to resolve, to not get stuck in the past, to see what the future holds. I would like you to experience what it actually means to inhabit the 'moving forwards' of which people speak.

Find yourself some space in a private place with some clear room ahead of you (about two metres is enough). Now visualise a situation in which you recently felt emotionally, financially or politically stuck or overwhelmed. This is your starting point. Envisage the situation in as much detail as possible.

Now very slowly take one step forward. What happens to the situation in your mind and is there a physical response? Do this a second time with a second step forward. And then again do it a third time.

After each step take a moment of reflection and make a mental note of what comes up for you. Try not to write anything down until you are at the end of the process and then notice what options or possibilities have presented themselves to you.

Note them down here:

_____

_____

_____

_____

Now jot down any emotional feelings that you felt as you walked forward along this invisible line. For example, did you feel apprehensive, did you feel relieved, or were there a range of emotions at different points? Again, spend some time to reflect and write these down:

_____

_____

_____

_____

There w.as likely some dialogue or optional responses as you went along the line too – things you may have said differently

Standing poses

The standing postures in yoga ensure that we are grounded and help us to connect physically with who we really are and be confident in that. To hold these standing postures for any length of time requires both stillness and strength within the body and mind. Again we can draw parallels with the assertive position – in order to hold the middle ground we need to be at a still and strong place to perceive the realities of what is going on.

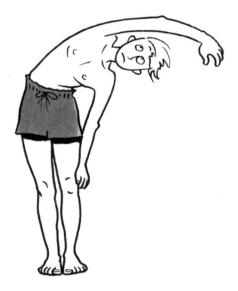

The Side Bend

Breathing and meditation

The breathing and meditation elements to yoga bring about a stilling of the mind and are therefore an excellent combative of stress and feelings of being overwhelmed.

They also allow the negative self-talk in our heads to wash over us more easily and allow a more objective viewpoint of the day-to-day, making it easier to employ assertive techniques and to raise our consciousness when we are slipping into an unhelpful emotional pattern. These practices tap exactly into the resources we need to give us the strength to make alternative choices.

The Cross-Legged Position

T'ai chi

T'ai chi is a practise of tuning into the different energies around us – through stillness and focus of the mind we can tune in to positive and negative energies, and with strong, specific bodily movements we can change that energy into something productive. It doesn't take much thought to see that we can extend this into the practices of assertive behaviour. We can take charge of the energies around us if we choose how we are going to respond to them. This is an empowering place to be.

Other sports and fitness

If we don't move we risk seeing things from a limited perspective and our emotions can 'get stuck' within our systems. It is these emotional sticking places that can lead to stress, resentment and illness. We literally stop 'moving forward.'

It is true to say that every sport or physical activity can help to tune us into our physical and emotional selves and the world around us in a strong and productive way. These physical activities allow our bodies to think as a more three-dimensional human being.

Those people who through illness or disability have limited movement options should ask advice as to what they can do safely. The goal is to physically move forward, whatever version is right for you.

Able-bodied people would do well to walk or run regularly at the very least. It needn't be a marathon and it will help with your assertiveness levels.

Posture and the Alexander Technique

Just like walking forward, standing in an aligned way is the perfect way for the body to become reunited with its true instincts and feelings and it can start to release those historical fears and traumas that are literally locked in the cells.

The only issue here is that the vast majority of us have grown up with people saying things like 'stand up straight' and us not actually knowing what that means. Often our version of this 'standing up straight' is a tense and held posture that is very different from allowing the natural skeleton to become aligned.

The Alexander Technique is an excellent place to start with this and can provide all sorts of solutions to a wide range of issues, physical and emotional.

More information on the benefits of this technique can be found at **www.stat.org.uk** and you can also source a local teacher there too.

Letting go of patterns

As we go through life, none of us remains unscathed by drama, trauma, hurt, loss and chaos at times. In order to get through these tricky times the body literally locks itself down, building a physical armour for the short duration it feels it needs it. The problem is that even when we are through these episodes in our lives, often the physical habit remains. This can compromise how effectively we respond to situations because it causes a disconnect in the physical body that consequently causes an emotional disconnect and therefore a lack of internal clarity. This muscle memory resides and so do the feelings, despite them now being redundant.

An example of this physical armour is a life-long habit I have in my neck and shoulders, for which I now need regular acupuncture and massage. It's a natural physical defence that kicked in for me as a youngster to protect myself from a range of situations and if it goes untreated for too long causes painful pins and needles in my hands. Now I am aware of it, I realise when my decisions are based on fear (influenced by a posture that creates a link back to a less secure time) or whether I need to stop to adjust my physical self before I make a more 'connected' and therefore confident decision.

When it comes to dealing with things assertively it can be these feelings that get in the way. Within them are fears about being hurt or traumatised again, and so we respond with fight (over-assertiveness), flight (under-assertiveness) or freeze (either), rather than feeling calm enough to rationalise the situation.

Write down all of the things you have gone through in your life that you feel you still 'carry something from' (be it something physical, like shoulder tension, mental, like being convinced that a certain 'type' of person means x, or emotional, such as being prone to tears easily or flying off the handle temper-wise):

_____

_____

_____

_____

_____

You will find that as you write this list some things will jump out at you as being your patterns of behaviour and it may be that these are now typical responses from you. The question is, are they useful for you? Are there any you would like to challenge or change?

It is crucial to note that this is not about being wrong, or giving yourself a hard time about the response. This is about understanding why and exploring the options around what can be consciously shifted so that you can assertively look after your own best interests and handle the challenges life throws at you with more strength and confidence.

brilliant exercise

Lie down, semi-supine, on the floor, with a couple of books to support your head if needed (see diagram below):

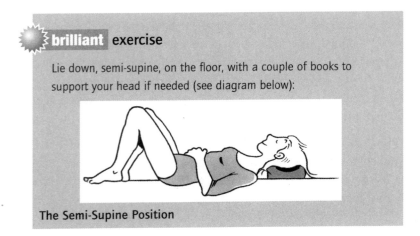

The Semi-Supine Position

Close your eyes and take some deep breaths out and in (always start with the out breath). Envisage your body sinking slowly into the floor – don't push, just allow. Think of yourself as a block of ice melting into the carpet or floorboards. Now guide your attention inwards and see if you can physically feel some of the tension areas you identified in your list above. Breathe into them and with the out breath imagine letting them go, imagine them drifting out to the sky like a balloon. Spend however long you need on each area.

Once you are done and you feel ready to stand back up, roll slowly onto your right side into a foetal position, then staying rolled up get onto your feet and slowly uncurl your spine, one vertebrae at a time, putting your head up last.

Now go back to your list of difficult scenarios and see if you feel differently about the response you had and how you feel you might respond now. Note down any differences. If we can work physically on the body, as well as psychologically, then we stand more chance of being able to move our behavioural responses into a more assertive place that serves us better.

brilliant recap

- Do practise doing things differently. It is not enough to just understand changes on a theoretical level; to start to become more assertive in your actions your body needs to get used to how it feels

- Always be aware of what other people are communicating by what they do and the effect their behaviour has on others, both positive and negative

- There are no fixed rules where body language and what it 'says' is concerned – it is all relative to specific situations

imperative to be clear about where you sit, even if you have no plans to divulge your thoughts.

So, take some time before any negotiation or deal to formulate your thoughts clearly and check how the deal sits within your own set of values.

Establishing the solid ground

What does the business want from this negotiation? Set an ideal, set something the business would be happy with and set the lowest possible acceptable thing.

IDEAL:

OKAY:

BOTTOM LINE:

Now check these with your own values and wants. What do you want from this negotiation ideally? What would you be happy with? And what is the lowest thing you'd settle for?

IDEAL:

OKAY:

BOTTOM LINE:

Are the two lists comparable, i.e. is there a link between each point where you can sit assertively and strongly, knowing your solid ground? Before you move any further forward in this nego-tiation preparation, this needs to be clear in your own mind in order to create the unshakeable ground that is essential for suc-cessful and assertive negotiation.

brilliant impact

Keeping it level

The next thing to be sure of is keeping the conversation level. If the person (or people) with whom you are in negotiation turns up their status in an attempt to have the upper hand, don't fight them or let it knock your status down. Just calmly hold your nerve (the equivalent of the adult state in Transactional Analysis) and repeat your point.

Say less

Don't over-talk. It's extremely common that in a pressured situation such as a negotiation, nerves can fuel the rambler in you. In these situations less is most definitely more. Say what you need to say in as few words as possible. Silently, though still pleasantly, hold the confidence in your point of view, which we have now established is unshakeable for you. Simply repeat your offer if you need to, in response to a push from the other side.

Of those who say nothing, few are silent.

Thomas Neiel, poet and photographer

What to do and what to say

Be interested in the other party. The information they give you is crucial to how you move forward. Not only this, but by listening to the other party you build trust and therefore a more effective negotiation ground. Ask further questions about their vision and point of view. Be specific and genuinely interested.

When time is an issue

If you need time, whether to consult someone else or just to check in with yourself to think things through, then state that you are taking it. Don't ask for it. Even if the negotiation is urgent, two minutes is doable. If you can, leave the room and walk for

> ### brilliant tip
>
> When you're next watching a TV interview or listening to a radio
> one, start to become aware of how the 'people dynamics' are
> playing out. Who does and says what and how does it affect the
> other person? This raises your levels of awareness about how we
> only ever do what we do as a response to something else. As
> human beings we are responsive creatures. Notice how this might
> compare to the effects people have on each other in a business
> negotiation.

Business meetings

One of the trickiest environments to be your own priority, first
and foremost, is the classic business meeting. Most of us are so
busy trying not to upset the apple cart and managing the big
personalities and hierarchical dynamics that we forget about our
own needs altogether.

Getting your voice heard

Even the most confident and assertive of us can suffer on this
front when there is a room of people discussing a very live issue
with degrees of passion. And in my experience there is nothing
more disheartening than leaving a meeting having not said anywhere near as much as you wanted to and feeling frustrated with
everyone, including yourself, about the way it was all managed.

So what's the main thing to consider? Give yourself the permission to interrupt. Not constantly, but when you really need to
get your point heard then slightly raise your voice above the row,
if you can. If this feels too scary then raise your hand and lean
forward until someone invites you in. You may still have to up
the volume on your voice a little when you finally do speak, but
at least the hand in the air and the physical movement make it

easier to get in. You will find that you leave the meeting far more settled than if you hardly said anything at all.

There are, of course, those meetings where you really don't have a strong enough opinion on the subject matter or you don't have anything to say. But say that, rather than nothing. Name what is going on for you with a sound level of assertiveness. You don't have anything to say and you one hundred per cent believe it so you can say it with confidence. Or agree with someone else's point, remembering to be specific and giving voice to it. 'Absolutely, Dave, I totally agree with your point about the team budget', gives a much clearer indication for people of what is going on in your head than saying nothing and them having to second-guess you. By giving your voice and what you have to say the same level of importance as everybody else's you are well on the way to treating yourself with a sound degree of self-respect.

Raising visibility

If you are new to a company, or people aren't that sure of who you are due to the company culture or suchlike, then it is probably time to realise that the responsibility to change things lies with you. It's time to get out those trumpets and blow them, it's time to shelve the modesty and it's time to not shy away too much from some limelight.

Using email and message boards to talk about what is happening in your world can be a great resource to start to raise your own visibility. Social media is better still. The likes of Facebook and Twitter are excellent (and if you think of yourself as a product to market and gain objectivity in that way, then you will be clearer about how to move forward). Internal communications such as Yammer are also excellent for social networking, general schmoozing, letting people know what you're working on, what hobbies you have and all sorts of other things, and again are fantastic for raising your visibility in the workplace.

Family matters and other personal relationships

When it comes to those we love, some people find it easy to be assertive and others find it harder. However it sits with you, though, there are a few key points to remember when dealing with those with whom the emotions run deeper.

Letting people know that you care

This one sounds fairly obvious but in actual fact we rarely give voice to this. Saying things such as, 'I know we don't always agree on stuff but I still care that you're okay', is a very productive and assertive way to build trust in treasured relationships.

Listening

Again this is one of the simplest things in life that we often forget, especially when we are stuck in patterns within households or familiar dynamics. Most of us know the power of listening and yet we still forget to do it day-to-day. If we really want to know and understand what is going on for the other person, listen to what they say.

brilliant tip

Think of listening as being like Stephen Covey's Talking Stick. This was an idea that Covey was introduced to by an American-Indian tribe and it goes like this: whoever has the stick (or other object) is the only person who can talk until they feel they have been understood. Nobody else can interrupt or put their viewpoint forward. Once the person feels understood, they then pass the stick to the other person involved. They do the same, again no interruptions. Even if you choose not to use the object itself you can envisage it, to start to train the mind to engage with and listen to what is being said, rather than jumping straight to your own position.

By listening to and therefore empathising with both or indeed all points of view in a given situation, compromise can be reached far more easily. Compromise is a powerful place to be because all points of view have been considered and then given an equal weight of importance.

The effects of taking on too much

Unfortunately this statement resonates loud and clear with many of us. So why do we take on too much in our lives? We may feel that we are responsible, or that it is just part of what is expected of us in terms of rules. It may be that our own goals and ambitions can be over-extended because we've always been a high achiever and able to accomplish almost anything and it is now part of our personal pattern. Or it may be that we struggle to simply say no, especially to those we love and care about.

It is important to have a reality check where this is concerned. Symptoms such as the common cold, IBS, migraine, anxiety attacks, depression, stress, chronic fatigue/ME, alcohol dependency/drug dependency, mood swings, insomnia, hormone imbalance, heart conditions and more have all been directly linked to a lack of assertiveness and not saying no even when we are stretched to our limit.

Think about the effects on your own health and your relationships with those you love if any of these conditions take effect.

If you find it hard to say no then just say yes to part of the task and negotiate the other part out. If you have always had a high bar for yourself simply lower it – chances are the lower bar is still an enormous achievement. If you have set rules for yourself then continue to challenge those rules to see if they are still serving you. Remember that everything we do and say in life is a choice that we are responsible for making.

Really? Can't we? Why not? What if we could have whatever we wanted? Then that is voluntarily taking a position of power, right? And that is really raising your head above the parapet and that can feel scary ...

But exciting? Come on it's exciting! We're going to go there! Yes, now.

> Whatever you do, or dream you can, begin it.
> Boldness has genius and power and magic in it.
>
> Johann Wolfgang von Goethe, writer, scientist and philosopher

Knowing exactly what you want

Goethe so wonderfully pinpointed it – dreaming it. We all day-dream, albeit some of us more than others. And we all dream in bed at night. Some dreams we recall on waking, some we recall later in the day all of a sudden and some we never recall at all. Start to keep a diary about all of the things you have daydreamed about, imagined or dreamed about during sleep. This diary need not go into detail or analysis. Notes are fine. After a week spend some time working back through what you have written and you will start to see some guidelines emerging. Our subconscious is incredibly clever at guiding us but we often don't trust it or take it seriously. For just one week I am asking you to listen to it. Think of it as an experiment.

Start to see what emerges here. For example, if I am preoccupied about a conversation I need to have with my agent and writing more books then that is my subconscious guiding me towards where I need to put some of my energies. At this stage it would be a good idea for me to start to jot this stuff down.

If I am daydreaming about being more impactful with what I say, with what I do and generally being more effective in how I com-municate within my profession with others, and so becoming more popular and creating more opportunities for myself, then that is what I am aiming for. It's what I want to happen. My subconscious is telling me what I need to know. By writing down how I envisage these conversations I can start to realise what I need to shift in my own behaviours in order to make them a reality for myself and so help to create the outcome I am choosing.

▶ brilliant example

Jaynie had always wanted to be a dancer. She loved it, fantasised about it on packed tube journeys through the city to and from her temp job, danced around her flat in her pyjama bottoms and was always singing the music from Tchaikovsky's *The Nutcracker* under her breath as she went about her day-to-day tasks. Even on a girls' night in she would get up and tiptoe elegantly across the room humming some classical ballet tune or other in order to retrieve a bottle of wine and top everybody up.

Her mother had never allowed her to go to dance classes as a child because they were 'too expensive' and, anyway, even if she could afford them they were 'too bourgeois.' So Jaynie never went, much to her disappointment and upset. She was encouraged to do 'more practical things' such as woodwork and learning to cook, which she obediently did, and was competent at, but never felt any real passion towards.

Then one day she rang me squealing with excitement. 'There's a dance school down the road and I have just enrolled! They accepted me!' It turned out she had been squirreling her money away for the last six months since the school had opened and had been practising like mad in her little flat to audition. The school took her predominantly because of her passion for and knowledge of dance, even though technically she still had a lot to learn. That was eight years ago.

Now Jaynie performs regularly as a dancer. Not for the Royal Ballet but for smaller-scale theatre shows. She rehearses a lot. Some would say she is very disciplined but in fact Jaynie simply loves to do it. She can't sit still so she'd ▶

What is your sphere of comfort within which to practise all of the assertiveness tools we have identified so far? And how do you ensure that you are working comfortably and productively within your own spectrum?

The important thing about assertiveness is to keep it authentic and adjust your own choices around communication to make sure that any tools or techniques you use serve you easily, without it feeling like you have simply added more things to the 'to do' list.

This is all about operating within your own personal spectrum of assertive behaviour and what is comfortable for you. Work with autonomy and you will find yourself in a pleasantly flexible and effective place.

Why bother changing anything at all?

Yes, even at this stage of the book this is worth asking. 'Why bother changing anything it all?' is a really important question because, actually, learning to be assertive and committing to implementing a more assertive existence for yourself means doing some work!

And it takes time. How many of us really have time available? And also, isn't it a little bit self-indulgent? I mean, we've managed this way so far haven't we? Is it really that important?

Well, yes, in short. You are the most important person in your world and you deserve this. And if you need reminding, go back to the introduction and re-read that.

It is important, though, to recognise that changing behaviours can feel terrifying because we equate that to changing who we actually are. We believe that if we start to shift our assertiveness levels we will be unrecognisable and we will lose all of our friends, family and anyone else close to us and have to start building relationships all over again. Not true. You are simply choosing to fine-tune your 'already-works-very-well-thank-you-very-much' self. Remember that you don't have to change much for people to realise that they cannot push you around anymore. And that can only be a good thing, right?

Identifying your own motivators

Do you know what motivates you? What are the things that might help to incentivise you to keep to your assertiveness goals and plans?

brilliant exercise

Think about something you did over the last week that you really enjoyed and describe it, explaining what you enjoyed about it here:

_____

_____

_____

_____

_____

_____

Now look again at what you have written and pull out the key words that tell you something about what you enjoy.

Here's an example:

'Last week I met up with a new friend. We went out and had a good chat about life and had a really good laugh. We had a great curry and some lovely cocktails and the night was just pure fun. We got on like a house on fire, we like the same music. I feel like I have met a friend for life.'

Okay what does that tell you about me? I like people, bonding, having fun, good food and drink, I also like music and love thinking things through and putting the world to rights, while having a laugh.

Because this is what I have chosen to talk about (and I did do a lot of other things last week besides this) then it gives you a good indication of what really motivates me.

So now, what motivates you?

_____

_____

_____

_____

_____

_____

And how does this translate into keeping you on track in terms of your assertiveness?

Using my example above, it is important for me to build good relations and understanding with people. Also, if I don't tackle any issues of work expectations being too huge on me, I will end up being resentful and destroying relations and the opportunity of bonding with people. So I am now really motivated to have that conversation with the people I feel are putting those expectations on me.

▶

That is what is important to me and motivates me. It may well be completely different for you but that doesn't matter. As long as you are using your own motivators from the derivatives above, then this exercise will work for you.

brilliant definition

Goal *n.* 1 The result or achievement toward which effort is directed.
2 aim. 3 end.

Keeping your goals in mind

It is the most important thing of all when developing within your own personal spectrum of assertiveness that you keep your goals clearly in mind. Even if you don't know what you want in terms of your assertiveness objectives then at the very least be clear what you don't want. Once you know this you can start to look at what the opposite might look or sound like.

It is important that you define your goal using positive language. For example, you may not want people taking advantage of you anymore but what would the opposite of this be? It might be that you want to be able to set some boundaries around what you are willing to take on and have people listen to what you are saying. If you are thinking about your manager in this situation focus on the latter rather than the former, which sits in negative language and therefore becomes an unclear goal. Focus on doing rather than not doing and keep the goal as specific as you can.

It is important to be situation-specific with the goal, as a piece of assertive behaviour in one situation may not map directly across to another. (For example how you choose to set boundaries around not taking on too much work from your manager may not look the same if you are setting boundaries around not doing too much in your role as a parent.)

State what you do want to achieve in terms of your goal or outcome below. Is your goal time-specific? When do you want to reach it by? Be clear with this too.

_____

_____

_____

_____

_____

_____

With goals, keep in mind that you are moving forward towards them – they lie ahead. As well as this, the goal must be something that feels doable to you. When you read back what you have written above there should be a sense within you of 'Yes, I really think I could make that happen', rather than 'Yeah, right, pigs might fly.'

For the goal to be reached successfully there needs to be a sense within you of how it would actually feel to be in that place. By connecting thoughts and feelings into what you want you are not only thinking your goal but experiencing it physically. As has already been pointed out in this book, everything within human beings is linked so the more holistically we can move forward, the more likely we are able to achieve our objectives. If we think assertively, we will act assertively.

By tuning in to how this goal feels we are also tuning in to our own internal communication channels, which will give us an alarm bell if we go off-track. We will 'just know' and be able to stop and redress the situation before we go any further, which is an extremely useful technique. It also means that we stick with the win-win in any given situation, as anything other would be counter-productive.

Monitoring and adjusting

When you are amid your journey to being more assertive it can be difficult to remain objective and take a step back in order to keep yourself on track effectively. Here are some tips that will help you to do just that:

1 Keep your attention on the impact your behaviour shifts are having on those around you. If you have only done a fraction of what you imagined you might have to do and you have achieved your desired outcome then be flexible and pull back. You need not go any further with this.

2 Give yourself credit. When you have managed to shift a way of thinking or a piece of behaviour, even if it has not yet had the desired effect, then take the time to recognise your efforts for yourself. Remember how difficult it is to even begin to think about assertiveness in a different way. If you are starting to actually behave differently around it then that is success indeed. Acknowledge that.

3 If things aren't working as you would like them to, then take some time to write out or jot down what has happened so far onto a piece of paper. By writing it out you are

effectively taking it out of your own head and putting the situation in front of your eyes, where you literally have a very different perspective. From there it should be easier to work out what has happened and what can be flexed in order to create a different impact.

Keeping yourself inspired

Inevitably there will be occasions, while working through your own personal shifts in assertiveness when you will think, 'Forget it! It's just too much hard work!' In moments like these it is useful to have some inspirational motivators to hand:

1   Go back to thinking about your own role models and what it is about them that you like so much and how their levels of assertiveness have served them.

2   Visualise the outcome. Notice how just by seeing this in your mind's eye your feelings, thoughts and general wellbeing are affected. This could be a day-to-day reality if you stay with your goals.

3   Check in with your own feelings along the way in terms of what is working for you and what isn't. Don't be afraid to modify behaviours using your own instinct if things aren't working as well as you might have hoped. Likewise, feel free to abandon things if they aren't working. Remember that there are no rules around assertiveness and that it looks very different for each and every individual.

4   Be careful you don't create a new list of rules around assertiveness for yourself and tenaciously keep doing something because you think it is a 'good' thing to do or that it is 'right.' Neither of these should be check-in points. Your one check-in point with yourself is this: is this working as I would like it to?

get what you want or there may be a compromise that emerges from a conversation and negotiation. Either way you have assertively influenced the situation.

Ensuring effective communication around assertiveness

Communication breaks down easily. When we talk to each other we tend to assume that everything that makes sense in our own heads is coming across exactly that way to the other person and that they understand things exactly as we do. Unfortunately this is usually not the case. We need to be aware of this when asserting ourselves and ensure that we are aware of the reference points for the other person involved, giving voice to them so that the other person is aware that we understand them.

We need to remain mindful of the other person's position and situation and give some acknowledgement about how they see the world, and we need to be able to convey exactly what we want to while including both points of view. It is no mean feat. It is a lot to remember to do, as well as get the clarity of your message heard and understood and establish your personal boundaries in a way that you haven't done before. So how do you go about it then? Let's break it down.

brilliant dos and don'ts

Do

✔ Take responsibility for how the information lands on the other person, as well as what you say

✔ Check with the other person that they are clear about what your intention has been

✔ Use questions (see next section)

✔ Change the way you convey your message if you think it may have been misunderstood

✔ Remember that everyone has a different life experience, which changes how they see the world and can often create misunderstandings; even people from the same family can be quite different in the way they interpret different behaviours

✔ Remember that facial expressions and tone of voice can help us to understand what somebody else is saying, along with the content of the message they are conveying

✔ Pay more attention to somebody's actions if what they are saying seems to be in conflict with what they are doing; their actions will be truer to how they really think

Don't

✘ Make an assumption about what the other person thinks based on their facial expression – check with them

✘ Assume that a word you use means exactly the same for another person (For example, where I am from, the North-East, 'canny' means lovely, in East London, where I live, it means a 'bit dodgy' and in Scotland it means shrewd, so I have to be clear and mention what I mean by it when having a conversation with someone from the South-East or North of the Border)

share these last-minute project requests with me from this point on? Am I right?' This type of question is excellent for ensuring that there is a clear understanding between people and is also great at diffusing conflict as it can help the other person feel they have been heard and that their point of view has been validated.

 He who trims himself to suit everyone will soon whittle himself away.

Raymond Hull, playwright, screenwriter and lecturer

brilliant recap

- Keep your assertive techniques in line with your own authentic style, only use the things that feel comfortable or doable and don't try to do things that feel way out of your comfort range

- Make sure that your goals are clearly defined and continue moving forwards towards them

- Keep in tune with your own internal signals – feelings, thoughts and instincts – on how things are going; know that you can rely on your internal system to keep you on track

- Take responsibility for setting your goal specifically and doing whatever needs to be done to keep yourself on track; be honest with yourself and always consider the range of options you have available

- Remember to check how your communications are landing with the other person – check in if you need to, use their terms of reference and acknowledge their point of view, or change tactics if you need to

- Hold your nerve on your decision if you genuinely believe you are on the right track; be sure to check in with the bigger picture so you can evaluate this objectively

Tips 'n' tricks

Simplicity is the ultimate
sophistication.

Leonardo da Vinci, artist and
polymath

The reality of it all

In actual fact, if we do not get straight to the point we risk several things happening:

1 People get irritated because they end up spending time and energy second-guessing what it is that you want to know/ask for.

2 If you do not ask you add to the hindrance of something getting resolved.

3 If you hesitate and put it off the issue can become bigger in your mind than in reality and so harder to deal with.

4 You may seem oversensitive and insecure so people avoid approaching you.

5 It can simply be irritating.

To illustrate the point, imagine you have been asked to present an award at the company's summer party and you feel very uncomfortable doing it.

If you were to answer in the following manner then imagine the effect it would have:
'I would really love to do it and I'm really touched that you're asking me but I am not sure whether I can actually make that date because I do have a lot on and I do need to check with my partner to see if they can manage the childcare that evening ...'

Now consider this option:
'It is so kind of you to ask. But I'm afraid I won't say yes because I'm too nervous presenting in public.'

Which would you prefer to be on the receiving end of? What would be your impression of the person delivering the second option to you as opposed to the first?

Taking time out

When you feel that a situation needs some head space, take it rather than ask for it. Communicate that's what you will be doing. Tell people you will be taking a couple of minutes/hours/ days/weeks to make a decision and don't be bullied into doing something quicker than you are comfortable with.

The same is true with turning off phones or limiting time with emails. If someone emails you at 2am and you respond straight away, the likelihood is that it won't be long before this just becomes expected behaviour.

Turn your email device off when you're asleep. Respond when it is convenient for you to respond. (NB I once worked with a woman who felt so pressurised into answering emails as they came in from her boss that she was answering emails while driving on the motorway! This is definitely not advisable for so many reasons.)

Holidays and any time you make for you are also key in this section. Think about the last time you took yourself away for a short break or even off for a half-hour back massage. Most people can come up with a whole load of excuses as to why they don't have the time or resources to do this but that is all they are – excuses!

Don't have the money? Go to a college where there are students studying beauty and they need people to practise on for just a few pounds. A hot bath doesn't cost much either. Or a long walk somewhere green.

Don't have the childcare? Find something relaxing you can do together, like a walk in the park, or ask a friend if they could take your little one for half an hour while you have a long bath or have a cat nap. Buy a running buggy (second hand) and take them with you for a run.

brilliant recap

- Fear is an illusion, it is not founded in reality, and the things we tend to fear rarely ever come true; and even if they do we are well equipped to deal with things, we just forget to believe that we are – believe it!

- If you have nothing to say then tell people that, rather than actually saying nothing

- Keep the 'issue' between you rather than either party picking it up and making it personal; by being objective about an issue and not taking it personally it is far easier to move forward productively

- Stop talking and park your point of view – simply listen to the other person as you cannot even begin to understand how things are for someone else if you do not listen to what they are saying; there is always plenty of time to put your own viewpoint across, it isn't a race

- Take the time you need to consider a matter and give an answer you are happy to give rather than leaping in and regretting it later on

- Don't say the word 'sorry' unless you have actually done something wrong and you seriously regret it; the word is over-used and it dramatically weakens your point of view

CHAPTER 11

Changing your assertiveness habits for good in 14 days

A truly good book teaches me better than to read it. I must soon lay it down, and commence living on its hint. What I began by reading, I must finish by acting.

Henry David Thoreau, author, poet and philosopher

smile. Take one interaction at a time and work through the day in detail. When you have got to the end of the day in your mind's eye, slowly open your eyes.

Now recall what you can about the short visualisation and record everything you can about those ideal successful interactions:

_____

_____

_____

_____

_____

_____

Follow up this visualisation by breaking the above down into no more than three key goals for the next 14 days. Remember that goals that are too big can often feel overwhelming and therefore end up not being tackled at all. (For example, if one of the exchanges on my list above is that I spoke to everyone with real authority and got everything I wanted, then I may want to shape this into a simpler and smaller goal and settle on just one or two influential people so that the whole thing feels more doable.)

Goal one: _____

Goal two: _____

Goal three: _____

Day one

At the start of the day

Look again at the first goal you have identified for yourself within this 14-day plan. Remind yourself of all of the reasons why you would like to reach this goal:

_____

_____

_____

_____

_____

_____

Identify all of the exchanges you are likely to have today that relate in one way or another to this goal:

_____

_____

_____

_____

_____

_____

What small thing/s (and identify no more than two here) can you realistically commit to doing today within these exchanges?

_____

_____

_____

_____

_____

_____

Day three

At the start of the day

Identify your strategy for the day. What conversations or actions do you have to take in order to move closer to your goal? This strategy might be that you are going to negotiate a workload with a colleague, initiate a conversation with your partner about a sensitive issue or it might be that you are simply going to reduce the amount of explanation you give in your day-to-day dealings. Outline below your commitment plan for the day:

_____

_____

_____

_____

_____

At the end of the day

Write some notes on the effects on others that you observed from adjusting your own behaviour and interactions:

_____

_____

_____

_____

_____

Day four

At the start of the day

Ensure that you are clear about what you feel your rights are within your own situations and what are the rights of the other people involved? (For example, you might feel that everyone has a right to express their views and everyone has a right to be listened to.) Identify these rights below:

_____

_____

_____

_____

_____

How can you ensure that these rights are acknowledged and enabled?

_____

_____

_____

_____

What can you actively do today to ensure that this happens, and in what situations?

_____

_____

_____

_____

Now that you can see that you are quite capable of dealing with the worst-case scenario, and remember that it is highly unlikely that it will happen, how does that make you feel?

_____

_____

_____

_____

_____

Day seven

At the start of the day

Simply make a mental note that today you will be taking some head space in order to recognise when people praise or compliment you. You will also be putting your attention on how to accept criticism in a constructive and confident manner so you can use it to continue to move yourself forwards towards your assertiveness goals.

During the day and at the end of the day

Make a note of any of this praise and criticism that has occurred throughout the day. How can you incorporate this into reaching your goals more effectively? (NB This may simply be that you allow yourself to hear and accept praise and criticism positively.)

_____

_____

_____

_____

_____

Day eight

Today your only task is to re-read your goals and make a mental note of what the last week has brought up for you. If you wish to write some things down then a space has been allocated for you below:

_____

_____

_____

_____

_____

Day nine

At the end of the day

Take some time to reflect and see if what you have remembered about the last week actually matches your notes. If there are some variations, however tiny, then this is a good time to notice how our human emotions and internal experiences of events can colour our memories.

Writing notes can help us stay accurate to what actually did happen, which can be a key tool in keeping us on track and linked into what is, rather than what we perceive it to be. The more in touch we are with exchanges and events as they occur, the more confident and assertive we can be in our responses to them, whether in the moment or afterwards. Note down any thoughts or observations you have concerning any of this:

_____

_____

_____

_____

_____

Day ten

At the start of the day

Write down any negative thoughts or self-talk that may be getting in your way on a daily basis:

_____

_____

_____

_____

_____

During the day

Challenge the list above, and any others that may come up, and treat them as questions that you do not have to answer rather than statements. For example, if one of the pieces of self-talk you identified above is, 'You're really not very good at this assertiveness malarkey!' then rephrase it for yourself into 'How do you think you are getting on with this assertiveness malarkey?' You will notice that the impact is quite different.

At the end of the day

Notice the effect of challenging the inner critic today and write down how it affected you and your behaviour:

_____

_____

_____

_____

_____

Day eleven

At the start of the day

Think about everything in this book that has stood out for you and you have thought, 'Oh I would love to try that with x situation or person.' Now select the top three that you would like to try but so far have felt a little wary about:

1 _____

_____

2 _____

_____

3 _____

_____

Now your commitment for today (or over the next three days if the relevant person/situation doesn't present itself today) is to see if you can try at least one of the above.

During the day and at the end of the day

Note down how this has all gone. Did you manage to act on any of the above? If so, what was the impact? If not, what was it that got in the way and is it something that you could actively influence in a different direction in the future?

_____

_____

_____

_____

_____

Day twelve

At the start of the day

Today is simply an opportunity for you to be with your own thoughts and feelings and allow them the space to exist, positive, negative or otherwise, without any judgement. If you catch judgement seeping in then let it go (visualise letting go of a balloon and allowing it to blow away out of sight). There is something incredibly powerful about just allowing ourselves to be with our thoughts and feelings without trying to push them away or chastise ourselves for having them. As far as confidence, self-esteem and assertiveness are concerned, once we stop battling with ourselves we feel more able and comfortable in acting upon what is right for us.

Note down anything you like related to this throughout the course of the day:

_____

_____

_____

_____

Day thirteen

At the start of the day

Today is the day to check in with where you are at so far with your assertiveness goals. Identify what has shifted for you to date:

_____

_____

_____

_____

Recognise what it is that you actively chose to do in order to create these shifts:

_____

_____

_____

_____

_____

Is there anything still outstanding that you would like to act upon in terms of further assertiveness development over the next couple of days?

_____

_____

_____

_____

_____

What strategies will you implement to achieve those last goals you have identified?

_____

_____

_____

_____

_____

Conscious competence

The individual has now grasped the skills needed and can perform them through choice, but at this stage there is some thought and effort required in the execution. The skill has not yet become an automatic thing and it needs practice in order for the brain and body to fully 'get it.'

Unconscious competence

The skill has now entered the unconscious part of the brain and is happening as second nature without any thought – it now feels instinctive.

As with most things, it is inevitable that this model will keep moving round. As one skill-set becomes unconsciously competent so another is moving from unconsciously incompetent to consciously incompetent. We may also start to raise our self-awareness to periodically consciously question our own 'unconscious competencies', and so the pattern continues again in order for the individual to further fine-tune their skills.

↗ brilliant impact

Simple, down-to-earth affirmations

Affirmations can get bad press. They can be perceived as fluffy, hippy-dippy, a bit daft and many other things. However, so long as they are simple and tangible they are incredibly powerful in terms of changing those not-so-useful thought patterns and negative self-limiting beliefs.

Here is a list of some of my favourite affirmations. It is important to choose something that resonates with your own unique set of circumstances, so feel free to adapt what is here or come up with your own:

● I am great just the way I am
● I am kind and thoughtful

- I am doing the best I can and that's more than enough
- I am at where I am at and that's okay
- It doesn't matter if things turn out differently from how I'd like them to
- I have enough life skills and experience to deal with whatever comes my way
- I am a human being and imperfection is to be celebrated
- Sometimes you've just got to let it go
- All that matters is the now and the future, the past has gone so there's no point in worrying about it
- I am lovely and I am going to let myself acknowledge that
- Go me, I rock!
- I love me, I'd be my mate!

brilliant recap

- Establish with clarity what you would like to achieve in your day-to-day life; be responsible for setting your own targets and keeping yourself on track with honesty and integrity
- Be sure to work with an awareness of the bigger and smaller pictures as much as possible, be aware of what is going on for others and be equally aware of what is going on for you
- Stay positive and proactive even when things may not turn out how you might have hoped
- Dedicate time for you – use this time to be kind to yourself and reflect on where you are for at least a few minutes at the beginning and the end of each day
- Allow yourself to be at wherever you are at; in other words, in both your professional and personal life, things go as they go and are easier to act upon when negative judgement is kept at bay

▶

- Re-frame any negative self-talk you become aware of as a question, not a statement of fact
- Keep moving forwards with pride

Conclusion

S o this is what 'assertiveness' is essentially all about. Once you make the decision to proactively change things for yourself in order to be more confident and achieve more in your professional and day-to-day life, there is really no going back. Once you are receptive to the fact that things can be different and you can be in charge of that, it is already a more confident and positive position to be operating from.

It is true that when we are not feeling assertive ourselves and we look at others, their way of operating can seem a million miles away and yet, once you begin to make just small shifts, then you really start to see the benefits. The key, as has been repeated in the book throughout, is to keep moving forward.

And, just to finish, there is one final note on handling other people's negativity:

If someone is negative towards you, either in what they do or what they say, if they put down you, the way you think or the values you hold, remember that it is their 'stuff', it is their own lack of self-esteem driving this behaviour and not yours.

If you choose to engage with their negativity, however, it becomes yours. If you give negativity any energy at all, it is given the chance to exist in your own life.

To come this far and engage with negative outlooks would be to go backwards. So keep your own self-respect intact. Ignore negativities where possible and, if you can, make a joke out of them. Resist the temptation to 'put down' in return. You don't need to. By rising above this sort of behaviour you are already holding your own assertiveness in high regard, and doing so will encourage other people to do the same.

Keep moving forward with resources

Below are some lists of web resources that you may find helpful in your assertiveness quest to move forward feeling confident, able and empowered.

Further web browsing

Assertiveness

www.assertiveness.org.uk

www.mindtools.com

www.teamtechnology.co.uk/assertiveness/how-to-be-more-assertive.html

Conflict and rules

www.angerplanet.co.uk

www.thefuckitlife.com

Fitness

www.fitness.com

Motivational

www.motivational-well-being.com

Running

www.fetcheveryone.com

www.runnersworld.com

www.runningforfitness.org

T'ai chi

www.everyday-taichi.com
www.taichiunion.com

Vocal resources

www.patsyrodenburg.com

Yoga

www.sivananda.org
www.yogabasics.com
www.yogajournal.com

Index

Goethe, Johann W. von 162
good assertiveness, examples
	15–18
Graves, Clare 72–4
Graves Value Model 72–4, 82
Guevara, Che 8

help, when you cannot 195–6
history of assertiveness, examples
	of public figures 7–9
holistic approach 136–9
home, rules in *see* rules of the home
Hull, Raymond 182
humming 117–18

imagery, use of when speaking
	114–15
intentions 127–8
interaction with audience 153
intimidation 5

Jolie, Angelina 30
Jonson, Ben 103

King, Martin Luther 115

language
	effects of 101–3
	limitations 111–12
	power of 115
life experiences, conditioning by
	xii–xiii
listening skills 151, 158
Long, Shelley 79

Madonna 147
mealtimes, toddlers 39
meditation 138–9
meetings *see* business meetings
monitoring and adjustment
	174–5
morals *see* values
motivators
	identifying personal 170–2

inspirational 175–6
multiple intelligences, theory of
	125

negativity, handling 193–4, 221–2
negotiation 149–52
	conversation level 151
	in day-to-day life 157
	listening skills 151
	overtalking 151
	personal values and needs
		149–50
	time pressures 152–3
	visualising good 152
Neiel, Thomas 151
nervousness 88, 89, 152–3
Nightingale, Florence 9

open questions 180–1
overly-assertive behaviour 7, 11,
	79–96
	assumptions 95
	on a date 87–9
	in restaurant 93–5
	when presenting 82–6
	in workplace 90–3

parents/guardians, rules of the
	home 44
passive choice 177
pauses, use of 113
perception of assertiveness
	models 9, 11
personal relationships 27–9, 158
	over-assertiveness on a date 87–9
pitching and presenting idea
	152–3
	interaction with audience 153
	structure 153
	see also presentation
point, getting straight to 188–90
	benefits 189
	fears 189
	reality 190